# PAR FOR THE COURSE

CW00552339

# PAR FOR THE COURSE
## by Peter Gordon

## JOSEF WEINBERGER PLAYS

LONDON

PAR FOR THE COURSE
First published in 2013
by Josef Weinberger Ltd
12-14 Mortimer Street, London W1T 3JJ
www.josef-weinberger.com / plays@jwmail.co.uk

ISBN: 978 0 85676 309 0

Printed by Commercial Colour Press plc, Hainault, Essex

To all frustrated golfers, golf widows and golf haters
... this play is for you!

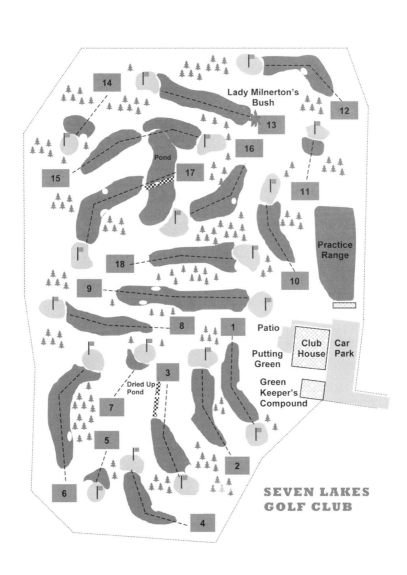

Lady Milnerton's Bush

Pond

Practice Range

Patio

Club House

Car Park

Putting Green

Green Keeper's Compound

Dried Up Pond

**SEVEN LAKES GOLF CLUB**

# SEVEN LAKES GOLF CLUB - SCORE CARD

| COMPETITION | CAPTAIN'S DAY COMP | | | | | | | | Ind Tee Used | |
|---|---|---|---|---|---|---|---|---|---|---|
| Date | ? | Time | 10.20 | | Handicap | | Strokes Rec'd | | Par 72 | |
| Player A | FRAN JEFFRIES (R) | | | | 8 | | | | Par 72 | |
| Player B | BARRY WEST (R) | | | | 28 | | | | Par 72 | |

~ICK                Score for statical purposes only!

| Marker's Score | Hole | White Yards | Yellow Yards | Par | Stroke Index | SCORE A | SCORE B | Nett Score | Points | Red Yards | Par | Stroke Index |
|---|---|---|---|---|---|---|---|---|---|---|---|---|
| 4 | 1 | 355 | 332 | 4 | 16 | 5 | 7 | | | 315 | 4 | 16 |
| 6 | 2 | 371 | 365 | 4 | 10 | 5 | 4 | | | 350 | 4 | 10 |
| 8 4 | 3 | 385 | 348 | 4 | 2 | 3 | 3 | | | 331 | 4 | 2 |
| 4 | 4 | 388 | 368 | 4 | 8 | 4 | 8 | | | 340 | 4 | 8 |
| 3 | 5 | 162 | 153 | 3 | 18 | 4 | 5 | | | 136 | 3 | 18 |
| Wasp 7 | 6 | 485 | 475 | 5 | 12 | 5 | 8 | | | 408 | 5 | 14 |
| 6 | 7 | 188 | 184 | 3 | 14 | 4 | 4 | | | 168 | 3 | 12 |
| 5 | 8 | 394 | 385 | 4 | 4 | 6 | 14 | * ? | | 372 | 4 | 4 |
| 5 | 9 | 560 | 542 | 5 | 6 | 4 | 7 | | | 406 | 5 | 6 |
| 44 | OUT | 3288 | 3152 | 36 | | 7 | 62 | 40 | | 2826 | 36 | |

PLEASE AVOID SLOW PLAY AT ALL TIMES

| 4 | 10 | 342 | 325 | 4 | 17 | 6 | 5 | | | 312 | 4 | 17 |
| 4 | 11 | 185 | 177 | 3 | 15 | 3 | 4 | | | 168 | 3 | 15 |
| 4 | 12 | 398 | 386 | 4 | 1 | 5 | 8 | | | 367 | 4 | 1 |
| 5 | 13 | 390 | 379 | 4 | 3 | 8 | 12 | | | 366 | 4 | 3 |
| Robb 4 | 14 | 208 | 202 | 3 | 7 | 3 | 5 | Neve | | 164 | 3 | 7 |
| 5 | 15 | 505 | 488 | 5 | 11 | 4 | 7 | parfav | | 423 | 5 | 13 |
| 6 | 16 | 344 | 325 | 4 | 9 | 5 | 4 | Barry! | | 315 | 4 | 9 |
| 6 | 17 | 498 | 480 | 5 | 13 | 4 | 7 | !!! | | 432 | 5 | 11 |
| 5 | 18 | 391 | 373 | 4 | 5 | 5 | 10 | | | 360 | 4 | 5 |
| 43 | IN | 3261 | 3135 | 36 | | 43 | 62 | | | 2907 | 36 | |
| 44 | OUT | 3288 | 3152 | 36 | | 40 | 62 | / | | 2826 | 36 | |
| (87) | TOT | 6549 | 6287 | 72 | | 83 | 124 | | | 5733 | 72 | |

| Stableford points or Nett result | | HANDICAP | 8 | 28 |
| | | NETT SCORE | 75 | 96 |

* Barry gives * £90

Markers Signature ...................   Players Signature ... J Jeffor

Remind Tiffs to obody sausages.

# CHARACTERS

| | |
|---|---|
| BARRY WEST | (40 to 55) Member of the golf club. Easy-going and good-natured but disorganised and unkempt. An enthusiastic but very poor golfer. |
| SIMON WEAVER | (40 to 55) Club Secretary. Fussy stickler for tidiness, rules, etiquette and gentlemanly behaviour. |
| NICK ARMITAGE | (40 to 50) Vice Captain. Generally amiable and well-meaning but cavalier with a take-it-or-leave-it attitude. Has a tendency to get occasional words wrong, often by inserting an unnecessary 'i'. |
| TIFFANY JENNINGS | (25 to 35) Nick's girlfriend. Younger than Nick. Not terribly bright but with a heart of gold. |
| FRAN JEFFRIES | (40 to 55) Ladies Captain. An attractive but rather butch and formidable woman who does not suffer fools gladly. |
| LAURA WEAVER | (40 to 55) Simon's long-suffering wife. |

The action of the play takes place on the patio and practice putting green outside the clubhouse bar of the Seven Lakes Golf Club.

The play can be easily adapted to any stage configuration and the course layout is intended to enable actors to visualise the position of 'on course action' referred to in the play.

Act 1 Scene 1:  A bright sunny Saturday morning.

Act 1 Scene 2:  Mid-day.

Act 2 Scene 1:  Mid-afternoon.

Act 2 Scene 2:  Early evening.

# ACT ONE

## Scene One

*The action of the play takes place on the patio and practice putting green outside the clubhouse bar of the Seven Lakes Golf Club and is well-suited for performance in any stage configuration.*

*The patio area is furnished with patio tables and chairs. A small section of the practice putting green is visible, with the rest of the putting green imagined to extend off stage. The external wall of the clubhouse can be seen, and contains a door that leads through to a bar. A sign over the door reads, "Seven Lakes Golf Club – Patio Spike Bar - No spikes permitted beyond bar". There are other stage exits from the patio area, leading to the car park and locker rooms and to various tees, greens and Green Keeper's compound. Some of these stage exits can be combined to suit the stage configuration.*

*It is a bright sunny morning, and* BARRY *is on the putting green. He is disorganised and unkempt and is dressed in scruffy golfing clothes of baggy shorts and a golf shirt, which is untucked at the front. He wears knee-length socks which are of slightly but noticably different colours. One sock is pulled higher than the other. He wears spectacles, which he tends to fiddle with nervously when stressed. He has half a dozen golf balls spread around him and stands over one of them with a putter, concentrating hard. After a few moments he takes the putt, sending the ball across the green and off stage.*

BARRY            (*watching the ball anxiously and talking to himself loudly and excitedly*) Hallo ... Come on, yes ... yes ... (*Frowning, disappointed.*) Ah! (*The faint sound of a Harley Davidson motorcycle can be heard from the car park area.* BARRY *glances toward the car park, raises his eyes heavenward and shakes*

*his head in disbelief before returning to
his putting practice. He moves to another
ball, about to take a second putt, then lifts
his putter up, looking at it suspiciously.
Pointing at the putter with his spare hand
and talking to it.*) Last chance, or you're in
the skip, mate. (*He positions himself over
another ball, lines it up and takes another
putt. He watches it closely again and leans
to his left, willing the ball to roll to the left.*)
Come round, come on ... come round ...
(*The ball clearly misses again and he snarls
at it loudly in frustration.*) Arghhhhh, bug–
(*He is about to hit the ground with the end
of his putter, but* SIMON's *entrance catches
his eye and he stops himself and moderates
his cry of anguish.*) ... bother!

(SIMON *enters from the bar. He is the Club
Secretary and a past captain of the club.
He is dressed immaculately in smart golfing
clothes and is a pompous stickler for
tidiness, rules, etiquette and gentlemanly
behaviour. He always has a notebook
and pencil with him to make small notes,
checklists and reminders. He is carrying a
small bundle of putting green flags.*)

SIMON       'Morning, Barry.

BARRY       'Morning, Simon. Looks like we've got the
            weather for it.

SIMON       Yes absolutely ... lovely ... (*Smiling with
            satisfaction as he gazes out front.*) Course
            looks a picture ... (*Frowning as he looks
            into the distance. Pointedly.*) ... apart from
            the new bloomin' bypass.

BARRY       To be fair, you can hardly see it.

SIMON        (*moodily*) I know it's there though,
             Barry ... I know. (*Glancing up at the sky
             suspiciously.*) Forecast for rain later.

             (SIMON *notices that some of the chairs are
             slightly out of position, sighs and moves
             them fractionally so that order is restored.*)

BARRY        Probably be brilliant all day then. You
             know what those weather bods are like ...
             couldn't predict snow in the middle of a
             blizzard.

SIMON        Quite. (*Finishing the chair repositioning
             and looking disapprovingly at* BARRY *and at
             an imagined collection of balls surrounding
             the hole off stage.*) Everything alright?

BARRY        No, not really. (*Holding up his putter in
             disgust.*) It's this thing. It's not right ... it's
             not right at all. (*Bitterly.*) I bought it off
             Nick.

SIMON        (*nodding sagely*) Enough said, Barry ...
             message received and understood. (*Every
             time* SIMON *says, "Message received and
             understood", he accompanies it with a
             little mime, tapping his index finger on
             his temple, then pointing it forward.*) Still,
             irrespective of that, the thing is ... as I
             came out ... (*Moving to* BARRY'S *side and
             speaking confidentially.*) ... just a word. We
             don't want to go upsetting the lady members
             again. I'll say no more ... don't want to
             labour the point. I'll just leave you with the
             thought ... language.

BARRY        (*bewildered*) What language? I didn't say
             anything bad.

SIMON        But it's the *way* you didn't say it, Barry.
             We just need to moderate the volume. I'll
             say no more. (*Looking around.*) Talking of
             Nicholas, any sign? He should be here by
             now.

BARRY        I think I heard him arrive a few minutes
             ago.

SIMON        (*glancing at his watch*) Typically late.
             (*Suddenly realising.*) Heard him? Not on
             that contraption!

BARRY        Sounded like it. Not one of his better buys
             but you know what he's like.

SIMON        (*bitterly*) Yes, I do. I think it's common
             knowledge that he wouldn't have been my
             choice for high office in the club.

BARRY        High office? It's not like he's been made an
             Archbishop or Chancellor of the Exchequer!
             He's only Vice-Captain.

SIMON        Captain next year though … ambassadorial
             position. In my opinion he sets a bad
             example to the membership. A man in his
             position needs to be beyond reproach …
             setting the required standard. Parking that
             machine in the official VC's  parking spot
             isn't on, Barry … it's just not on.

BARRY        It's usually more of a semi-controlled
             keel-over than a park. Bit of a danger to
             everyone.

SIMON        Exactly … and my bay is next to his.
             (*Thoughtful.*) I may have to re-allocate
             spaces so he parks next to someone else.

| | |
|---|---|
| BARRY | (*sarcastically*) Good idea, Simon. You've always been a good team player. |
| SIMON | (*absently*) Right. (*Checking his notebook.*) I need to appraise Nicholas of the current situation vis-à-vis today's itinerary. (*With a martyred expression but clearly trying to conceal his delight.*) Grave news from the Captain ... looks like I'll be called upon to shoulder the burden of responsibility I'm afraid. |
| BARRY | Why, what's happened? |
| SIMON | All in due course, Barry. I need to inform the key personnel first. Let's just say there's been a critical development ... enough said? |
| BARRY | Well, you usually *say* enough, Simon. It's just that the sentences rarely contain much useful information. |
| SIMON | Mmm ... (*Noticing* BARRY'S *socks.*) Socks, Barry! |
| BARRY | What about them? |
| SIMON | They're not a matching pair. Club rules clearly stipulate ... |
| BARRY | Well, they were sold to me as a pair. In fact, I've got an identical pair at home. |
| SIMON | Give me strength! And your shirt. Something wrong with your shirt? |
| BARRY | (*glancing down at his shirt*) Don't think so. Probably due a wash ... I do it once a season whether it needs it or not. |

SIMON            (*exasperated*) You're all untucked, man.
                 Practically exposing yourself!

                 (BARRY *thrusts his putter into* SIMON'S
                 *hands and reluctantly tucks the front of
                 his shirt into his trousers but, in doing so,
                 inadvertently untucks it at the back.*)

                 (*passing the putter back to* BARRY)
                 Standards, Barry ... that's what sets us
                 apart from the common rabble. (*Noticing
                 that* BARRY'S *shirt is now untucked at the
                 back and sighing heavily.*) I don't know why
                 I bother! (*Glancing down at the flags in
                 his hand and frowning at* BARRY.) Right ...
                 you'll have to come off there.

BARRY            But I was practicing. That is allowed isn't it?

SIMON            Not at this precise moment in time, no.

BARRY            But it's the practice green!

SIMON            Not when the flags are out of the holes it's
                 not. When the flags are *in* the holes you
                 can use it ... when they're not, you can't
                 ... at the moment the flags are out, so it's
                 currently inoperative.

BARRY            Why?

SIMON            Because the flags are *out*. Come on ... let's
                 have you off.

BARRY            But I demand to use the facilities. I'm a
                 fully paid up member.

SIMON            (*physically ushering* BARRY *off the green*)
                 I don't care if you're a member, the Queen
                 of Sheba, or Tiger bloomin' Woods. The

flags are out and the Head Green Keeper has entrusted the organisation of the putting green to me. Out of my hands I'm afraid ... regulations.

(NICK *enters from the car park. He carries an open-faced motorcycle helmet and is dressed in jeans and a tasselled motorcycle jacket. He is well-meaning but cavalier and has a tendency to get occasional words wrong, often by inserting an unnecessary 'i'.* NICK *and* BARRY *are good friends and there is always friendly rivalry and banter between them.*)

NICK  (*cheerfully*) Now then, stand by your beds. Alright there, Bas ... Simon.

(SIMON *looks* NICK *up and down with clear distaste.*)

What's wrong with you? You've got a face like a wet weekend. (*Adopting a heavy German accent.*) Did von of ze members forget to salute you, mein Fuhrer?

SIMON  You're well aware of my views on you leaving that motorcycle in the members car park ... it's hardly appropriate.

BARRY  (*chuckling to himself*) I thought it was a Hardly *Davidson* ...

(SIMON *remains stony-faced.*)

*Hardly ... Davidson* (*Moving to sit at one of the tables.*) ... never mind ... suit yourself.

NICK  (*indignant*) Actually, Barry, it's *Harley.*

BARRY                I know!

NICK                 A 'Harley Davidson Fat Bob'.

                     (TIFFANY *enters from the car park. She is*
                     *much younger than* NICK, *tartily dressed*
                     *and teeters on high-heels. Although not*
                     *terribly bright, she has a heart of gold, and*
                     *is practicing to become an air hostess. She*
                     *usually speaks with a blunt and common*
                     *accent but occasionally makes a conscious*
                     *effort to adopt a rather false, drawn out*
                     *and whiney 'air hostess voice' which she*
                     *uses when she is trying hard to be pleasant*
                     *or impress. She is also trying to develop a*
                     *helpful smile but often adopts it at totally*
                     *inappropriate moments. As she enters she*
                     *is half carrying, half dragging a shabby*
                     *folded patio table behind her.*)

TIFFANY              He couldn't get one called 'big fat lazy
                     slob', could you Nick?

                     (SIMON *glances round at* TIFFANY *and then*
                     *does a horrified double take as he sees*
                     *what she is wearing.*)

SIMON                (*to* NICK) Who's that?

NICK                 (*innocently*) I don't know. To be honest,
                     I think she must be a stalker … she just
                     followed me.

SIMON                (*to* TIFFANY) This is a private club, young
                     lady. If you're on trades-persons business
                     you'll need to ring me. (*Pompously.*) I'm
                     the Secretary but just plain Mr Weaver will
                     suffice.

(TIFFANY *stops and wipes her brow as she looks at* SIMON *in disbelief.*)

TIFFANY    Nick told me about you! Hi Barry.

(BARRY *smiles back and gives a little wave as* TIFFANY *starts dragging the table again.*)

NICK    Hey, you be careful with that. That's my best patio table.

BARRY    You mean you've got one *worse* than that?

TIFFANY    He's been going on at me all morning, Barry. It's like, do this ... do that. (*To* NICK.) If it's so precious you can carry it yourself.

SIMON    (*to* NICK) She *is* with you?

NICK    Of course she's with me. (*To* TIFFANY.) Say hello to Simon ... he's not much to look at but he has got plenty of money.

TIFFANY    (*moving to* SIMON) Hello, Simon. I'm Tiffany ... (SIMON *instinctively holds out his right hand and* TIFFANY, *mistaking his actions, thrusts the table at him so he has to take it.*) ... but plain Miss Jennings will suffice. And actually, I'm an air hostess.

NICK    No you're not.

TIFFANY    I nearly am. (*To* SIMON.) I've submitted several applications and attended a preliminary interview.

NICK    They said she'd have to improve her dictation.

TIFFANY     Diction, Nick! And they said I should try to
            smile more. (*Giving a false smile and then
            turning to* NICK *and adopting 'air hostess'
            speech and mannerisms, miming with her
            arms.*) Would you care for this table to be
            placed in the upright or the user position?

            (SIMON *scowls, rests the folded table against
            one of the chairs and then exits across the
            putting green as he goes to place the flags
            in the holes.*)

NICK        Tiffs, will you stop messing around and just
            go and get the rest of the gear from your
            car.

TIFFANY     But the car's packed with stuff! Aren't you
            going to help?

NICK        Help? How can *I* help? I need to get
            changed. I'll see if I can spare Barry for
            you later.

BARRY       Me!

NICK        Stop you hanging round like a spare part for
            a change.

TIFFANY     (*muttering*) He couldn't even be bothered
            to help me load up at the other end. I was
            supposed to be going shopping today.

NICK        You *always* go shopping on Saturday.

TIFFANY     That's because I *like* shopping, stupid. It's
            my hobby.

NICK        Well you ought to thank me ... I'm saving
            you a fortune. (*Moving to* TIFFANY *and
            giving her a peck on the cheek.*) Alright? So

let's not get all aer-i-ated about it, eh? Now,
off you go. If you're good I'll get Simon to
fix you up with a complimentary pitch mark
repairer.

TIFFANY        (*grumbling as she exits to the car park*) You
               do my head in, Nick, you *so* do my head in.
               I always end up doing everything.

NICK           (*watching her, sadly*) She's got her uses but
               she's very high maintenance. Very hormo-i-
               nal. Lovely arse though.

               (SIMON *enters across the putting green,
               having completed placing the flags.*)

SIMON          She's not staying is she? Not dressed like
               that.

NICK           Looks alright to me.

SIMON          Standards, Nicholas. Point taken? Right,
               Barry … you can practice now.

BARRY          What?

SIMON          Flags are in. The putting green is back on-
               line.

BARRY          So why did you make me come off?

SIMON          Flags were out.

BARRY          Heaven help us! By the way, Nick, this
               putter's crap … I want a refund.

NICK           More chance of Nelson getting his eye back.
               No fallen darts returned and all that.

BARRY          But according to 'Golf Monthly', I shouldn't
               be able to miss with this particular model.
               (*Examining the putting blade suspiciously.*)
               Have you stuck the end back on this?

NICK           (*looking guilty*) And why would I do that?

BARRY          Well, you're always throwing your clubs
               at things ... you're the grumpiest golfer I
               know!

NICK           Rubbish. Operator error, Barry ... that's
               your problem.

               (BARRY *looks at the putter suspiciously
               again as he moves back to the putting
               green and begins to practice his putting
               again. During the following passage,
               he tries a variety of putting techniques,
               shutting his eyes, changing his stance, etc.
               Occasionallly he disappears from view, off
               stage, as he goes to retrieve his golf balls.*
               NICK *spots someone off, down right, and
               waves.*)

               (*Cheerily.*) 'Ey up, Bob? Missus let you out
               today then? ... (*Wincing as he receives an
               unheard response.*) Sorry, there's no need
               to be like that ... I didn't know. (*Brighter.*)
               Still, you'll be able to get a few more games
               in now. See you later. (*To* BARRY.) I'm not
               surprised she's left him, miserable old
               bugger. You do well to stay single, mate.

BARRY          Nobody'll have me. Don't know what
               Tiffany sees in you.

NICK           Ah well ... (*Wiggling his hips.*) Sex machine
               me, Bas ... I've always been a bit of a babe
               magnet.

| | |
|---|---|
| SIMON | (*to* NICK, *suspicious*) So, what's the table for? |
| NICK | Eh? Oh, I told Jeff I'd sort out a halfway house. The plan is ... people come off after the ninth and Tiffs serves them a sausage sarnie and a smile before they tackle the back nine. |
| SIMON | (*taking his notebook from his pocket*) What? Oh no, no, you can't do that. I'll have to check with the club caterer. |
| NICK | Who doesn't give a stuff 'cos I've already asked him. He's up to his eyebrows in prawn cocktails and brocc-i-oli, getting ready for the dinner. |
| SIMON | (*writing in his notebook*) Not been approved ... I've made a note. |
| NICK | Well, to be honest, it's none of your business. It's Captain's Day ... which means it's Jeff's day. |
| SIMON | (*triumphant*) Not any more it isn't. Jeffrey's rung in sick so I'm re-evaluating the plans. |
| NICK | Sick? What's wrong with him? |
| SIMON | That doesn't matter. On a strictly need to know basis, you don't need to know. |
| NICK | Yes I do. I'm his Vice. |
| BARRY | Not his only vice from what I've heard. |
| | (BARRY *takes a practice putt but strikes the ground several inches behind the ball. He taps the green guiltily, hoping that no one* |

                        *has noticed.* SIMON *pulls* NICK *aside so that*
                        BARRY *can't hear.*)

SIMON                   (*confidentially*) For your ears only. His
                        wife rang me first thing this morning and
                        said that's he's under the weather. She
                        wasn't prepared to go into specifics but I
                        got the impression that it was an ailment
                        of a personal nature, so I didn't press her.
                        Enough said?

NICK                    (*grinning*) Well, that puts *me* in charge then!

SIMON                   No it doesn't. I'm Club Secretary and I have
                        reluctantly stepped into the breach.

NICK                    And I'm Vice Captain and I don't give a
                        bugger what you've stepped in. This is
                        Captain's Day and I'm second in the chain
                        of command after Jeff.

SIMON                   (*blustering*) Ah, but I'm a *past* Captain. It
                        clearly states in the club's constitution that
                        I take seniority in a crisis.

NICK                    Prove it.

SIMON                   Well ... ah, it may not say it in black and
                        white but ... (*Thoughtful.*) the Secretary
                        would have to clarify it and, seeing as I *am*
                        the Secretary I think that wraps things up
                        quite nicely.

                        (TIFFANY *enters stage left, carrying a large
                        cardboard box.*)

NICK                    (*prodding* SIMON *with his finger*) I'll wrap
                        *you* up in a minute, pal. Listen, it's Captains
                        Day ... I am now formally degl-i-gating

                    myself in charge, so you can stick that up
                    your constitution!

TIFFANY             You're not arguing again are you, Nick?
                    You're always arguing.

NICK                No, I'm not. I'm just making a stand for
                    demography.

TIFFANY             (*placing the box on a table*) What is
                    Captain's Day anyway?

NICK                (*exasperated*) I've explained it to you three
                    times!

TIFFANY             See ... you're arguing again!

NICK                No, I'm not arguing ... (*Gently.*) I'm just
                    pointing out that you're thick.

TIFFANY             I can't help it ... and actually I'm not
                    anyway ... you're the one who always gets
                    his words wrong.

BARRY               (*as he continues practicing*) Captain's Day
                    is one of the big events in the club's year,
                    Tiff. The Captain and Lady Captain set the
                    competition off by driving up the first.

TIFFANY             Doesn't that make a mess? Is that why you
                    wanted to come on your bike, Nick? Are
                    you using that?

NICK                (*sitting down, exasperated*) He doesn't
                    mean driving a vehicle does he!

TIFFANY             How am I supposed to know?

SIMON               (*sulking but unable to resist*) Driving is
                    a technical term for propelling the ball

off a tee, normally with a driver or other wooden club, which these days is, in practice, usually a *metal* wooden club with a composite carbon fibre shaft.

TIFFANY     You what?

BARRY       And normally making a complete pillock of yourself when the ball only goes five yards.

SIMON       (*formally, as though giving a presentation*) Here at the Seven Lakes Golf Club, the day traditionally consists of a combined mixed pairs and individual competition for all *full* members and ladies ... five-day members excluded ... followed by a four course Captain's dinner, prize-giving and dance.

TIFFANY     (*pulling a face*) Lovely. Anyway, my Dad says he wouldn't join here if you paid him.

SIMON       Yes, well, we do have very strict criteria. Perhaps your father feels embittered that he wasn't granted the privilege of membership at some stage in the past.

TIFFANY     It can't be that strict ... you let gobby Nick in!

NICK        Hey you ... just watch yourself.

TIFFANY     Anyway, he never wanted to join. So why's it called the 'Seven Lakes Golf Club' then?

SIMON       (*condescendingly*) Because of the seven lakes around which the course was originally contoured.

TIFFANY     Dad says there were only ever two small ponds.

PAR FOR THE COURSE

| | |
|---|---|
| SIMON | Ah, yes ... but the founding fathers rather felt that 'seven lakes' more accurately reflected the aspirations of the club. |
| TIFFANY | And he says that one of them's dried up. |
| SIMON | (*irritated*) Your father seems to know a great deal! We're currently in dispute with the local Council and the Highways Agency. (*Glaring at* BARRY.) When *Barry* here built the new by-pass, he failed to spot that the drainage works would affect our water table. |
| BARRY | I didn't build it on my own ... I was only doing my job! |
| SIMON | And left us with a huge empty pit. |
| BARRY | Well, just fill it up with sand then. The 'Dirty Great Bunker and a Duck Pond Golf Club' has a certain magical ring to it. (*Putting another ball and complaining.*) I've not got *one* in yet, Nick! |
| NICK | You could always try aiming for the hole. (*Standing, decisive.*) Right ... due to Jeff's absence I'm now the acting Captain. Tiffs, you need to get your skates on. |
| TIFFANY | Why? |
| NICK | You're on your own ... I can't spare Barry now. |
| TIFFANY | But I don't know what I'm supposed to be doing! |
| NICK | Ah, well, situation normal then. It'll be good practice for being a trolley dolly. |

TIFFANY          (*indignant*) We're not called that, Nick.
                 We're officially called Cabin Crew, actually.

NICK             Yeah, whatever. (*To* BARRY.) Bas ... with me.
                 We need to get things set out for the longest
                 drive and nearest the pin competitions.

SIMON            You can't go on the course dressed like
                 that!

NICK             No? Just watch me. Come on Barry.

                 (NICK *and* BARRY *move to exit onto the golf
                 course.*)

SIMON            Shirt, Barry.

                 (BARRY *shuffles off behind* NICK, *tucking his
                 shirt in at the front.*)

BARRY            What's wrong with Jeff then?

NICK             Pox.

SIMON            (*shouting after them.*) I never said that!

TIFFANY          (*shouting after them*) Nick ... you haven't
                 told me what to do! Nick! (*To* SIMON.) He *so*
                 does my head in.

SIMON            He does my head in as well, Tiffany! Fair
                 comment. Point taken ... message received
                 and understood.

                 (*A mobile phone rings loudly in* SIMON'S
                 *pocket. He looks around fiercely, ready
                 to admonish the member who has left a
                 mobile phone switched on. Seeing no one,
                 he guiltily realises that it is his own phone
                 and takes it out of his pocket. He looks*

*around to see if anybody has noticed and sees* TIFFANY *watching him.* SIMON *smiles weakly at her, shrugging his shoulders and pointing stupidly at the phone, before peering anxiously at the phone to read who is calling him. Reading the caller's name he grimaces and reluctantly presses a key to receive the call. He adopts the posture of someone who knows he shouldn't be using the mobile phone, making himself look as small and inconspicuous as possible. Throughout the call,* TIFFANY *pretends to look through the contents of the cardboard box but she is clearly listening to the phone conversation.*)

SIMON                    (*speaking into the phone*) Hello my love ...

                         (SIMON *winces as he obviously receives a fierce tirade from the caller. He smiles in a conciliatory way, as though the caller can actually see him.*)

                         ... no, of course not, no ... nowhere near the golf club ... (*Wincing again, he looks down at his clothes.*) ... Well, they were all I could find to put on so I thought they'd do ... (*With a flash of inspiration.*) in fact I'm just in B and Q researching satin gloss ... it seemed an ideal opportunity because you said a colour like my golf top might be rather nice ... (*Frowning.*) It's what? ... well, where's the water coming from? ... Well, you'll just have to get a plumber in ... (*Wincing again.*) That sort of language isn't very helpful, Laura ... No, not a chance. Look, have to dash because one of my clients has rung and I need to see him urgently so I'm rather snookered ... all day and evening I'm afraid, so (*Cheerfully.*) good luck with the leak ... (*He holds the*

*phone away from his ear as a tirade of
abuse hits him.*) But I can't ... Laura? ...
Laura?

(SIMON *switches the phone off and replaces
it in his pocket. He glances around guiltily
to see if anybody has noticed his phone call
and he sees* TIFFANY *still watching him.*)

(*Smiling weakly.*) Seems we have a leak.

TIFFANY        Oh?

SIMON          In the downstairs cloakroom ... and halfway
               down the hall ... just flowing through into
               the lounge now apparently. Just as well
               we've not decorated yet. Small to medium
               tsunami by the sound of it.

TIFFANY        (*sympathetic*) Gets everywhere does water
               ... unless it's in a pipe ... or a bucket.

SIMON          Not been moved long. Wife's idea. We
               haven't quite got round to re-painting and
               the like.

TIFFANY        I'm not sure I'd go for *that* colour myself.

SIMON          What? Oh ... the top? (*Glancing down at his
               shirt.*) I think it was the other one she liked
               actually. (*Embarrassed.*) You may have
               heard me mention B and Q ...

TIFFANY        Yeah?

SIMON          Just having a bit of a joke with the wife.
               Wouldn't want you to think ... you know.

TIFFANY        Nothing to do with me.

SIMON        No, I suppose not. Not at all. Fair comment.

TIFFANY      No harm in a bit of a fib now and again
             though. I sometimes tell the odd little white
             one to Nick.

SIMON        (*understanding*) Ah.

TIFFANY      Nothing like the bloody great lies he
             tells me though. He *so* does my head in
             sometimes! Still ... (R*e-focusing.*) I thought
             those weren't allowed.

SIMON        What?

TIFFANY      Mobile phones. Nick hid mine. (*Miming
             thumbing a text message.*) He says if I had
             my thumbs cut off I wouldn't survive more
             than a day.

SIMON        No, they're not allowed ... club rule 17b ...
             (*Hurriedly but unconvincingly.*) but I'm the
             Secretary.

TIFFANY      (*confidentially*) Tell you what ... put it on
             vibrate, nobody'll know. I won't tell anyone.

             (TIFFANY *smiles at* SIMON *and then exits to
             the car park.* SIMON *watches after her.*)

SIMON        (*to himself*) Extraordinary woman.

             (SIMON *takes the mobile out of his pocket
             and fiddles about with it, changing the
             ring tone. There is a bellow from the Lady
             Captain,* FRAN.)

FRAN         (*off*) Ah, Weaver ... there you are.

(SIMON *is clearly horrified at the arrival
of* FRAN *and quickly puts the phone away
in his pocket.* FRAN *enters from the golf
course. She is an attractive but formidable,
'no nonsense' woman, who appears to be
fully prepared for any challenge that life
might throw at her. She is dressed in golfing
clothes.*)

FRAN            'Morning, Weaver. Bit late out of the blocks
                this morning weren't you? I've been on the
                practice range since eight. I hear there's a
                spot of a crisis.

SIMON           No, not really. Laura's got a problem with
                the plumbing, that's all. Bit of a pain but
                hardly life threatening.

FRAN            Oh … a dose of antibiotics will soon sort
                that out. Seems like the chaps' skipper's
                in a bad way though. (*Laughing heartily.*)
                Been mixing with the wrong type of girl
                from what Armitage tells me.

SIMON           Nicholas? I never told him that!

FRAN            Don't worry, I won't breathe a word.
                Anyway, seems like Armitage and I
                are running the show now, so we'll be
                teeing our fourball off together at ten
                hundred hours sharp. (*Looking at* SIMON
                *appraisingly.*) Now … a quick word.

SIMON           (*blustering*) Ah … bit busy actually.

FRAN            Nonsense. (*Forcing* SIMON *into a chair.*) As
                Ladies Captain I intend to use my year to
                resolve all of the outstanding issues relating
                to the girls.

| | |
|---|---|
| SIMON | Issues? Oh no, I don't think there are any of those. |
| FRAN | Don't be ridiculous. I clearly set out the main points in the letter I gave to you last week. |
| SIMON | Ah yes … your letter. |
| FRAN | You have read it I trust? |
| SIMON | (*smiling at her with an embarrassed and apologetic expression*) I'm afraid I had a shredding accident in the office. A number of valuable documents were inadvertently destroyed … including your letter I believe.<br><br>(NICK *and* BARRY *enter from the golf course, arguing with each other.* BARRY'S *shirt is now untucked at the back again.*) |
| NICK | I've got enough to think about, Bas … seeing I've been dropped in it. |
| BARRY | But how was I to know you'd left all the equipment in the locker room? I'm not psychic! (*To* SIMON *and* FRAN.) He's losing the plot. (*Sitting.*) He's worse than my Aunt Mary and she doesn't even know who she is! |
| NICK | Well, maybe if you *were* a bit more psychotic you'd be useful for a change! Have you ever thought of that? |
| FRAN | Fortuitous that you're back, Armitage. You and West can support my demands for justice for the ladies. |

SIMON            I don't think this is the appropriate time, Frances. I need to organise the day's proceedings.

NICK              No you don't. Anyway, to be honest, your idea of organising anything is to degl-i-gate it to everyone else, so we're better off without you.

FRAN              Point number one. It's simply not acceptable that the ladies are restricted to playing between eleven hundred hours and noon two days per week.

SIMON            But you're allowed to play today.

NICK              And anytime after dark.

FRAN              (*scowling*) Point two. We demand to be allowed to use the front door of the clubhouse again.

SIMON            But if I may remind you, we introduced the ladies rear entrance rule three months ago to *accommodate* the wishes of the ladies section.

FRAN              Oh, I freely admit that several of the more delicate ladies did complain about bad language coming from the men's locker room, but banning us from walking past it was hardly a fair solution!

SIMON            It *was* agreed by a majority vote of the Facilities Committee.

                        (SIMON *attempts to stand to signify that the conversation is ended.*)

FRAN            (*moving towards* SIMON *determinedly*)
                Which is dominated by men.

SIMON           (*intimidated, rapidly sitting again and
                shrugging*) Out of my hands.

FRAN            Nonsense. Point three. We demand that the
                large ornamental shrub be removed from
                the front of the thirteenth tee.

SIMON           But that was donated by our very first
                honorary lady member in 1923.

FRAN            But it's now twenty feet high and only ten
                feet in front of the ladies' teeing area. None
                of the ladies can ever clear it!

SIMON           We  have an annual trimming programme.

FRAN            And it keeps growing even faster. It's
                like a triffid! Mrs Bickersdale went in to
                retrieve her ball and had to be cut out by the
                greenkeeper.

SIMON           In any case, the Greens Committee has
                just decided to name all of the holes on the
                course. That shrub is the signature feature
                of the thirteenth.

BARRY           Personally, I don't think calling it Lady
                Milnerton's Bush is a very good idea!

SIMON           That's *not* what was decided!

BARRY           (*confused*) But Nick's got the sign made up
                ready.

NICK            Oh, thank you very much, Barry ... that was
                meant to be a bit of a joke for today! There's
                no need to go round telling everybody.

BARRY            Well, *I* didn't know!

                 (TIFFANY *enters from the car park, carrying
                 another large cardboard box.*)

FRAN             (*to* SIMON) There are several other minor
                 demands. I'll let you have a note of them
                 later. (*To* NICK.) I trust that I'll have the
                 full backing of our men's Vice Captain?
                 (*Puzzled.*) Why are you dressed like a
                 cowboy?

TIFFANY          Nick reckons it makes him look cool. In my
                 opinion it just makes him look like a sad old
                 git.

NICK             But we didn't ask for *your* opinion, did we?

TIFFANY          No, I'm just the gofer ... sorry I spoke. (*The
                 bottom of the box suddenly falls open and
                 several plastic bags, clearly containing
                 something 'squashy' like meat and pies, hit
                 the ground with a dull thud.* TIFFANY *pulls a
                 face.*) Oops ... hope that wasn't important!

                 (NICK *looks to the heavens in despair.*)

                 There's another six boxes to come ...
                 (TIFFANY *looks around hopefully for
                 volunteers but gets no reaction.*) ... so a
                 hand would be quite useful.

NICK             I've told you ... I'm busy.

SIMON            (*hurriedly*) And I have rather a bad back,
                 I'm afraid.

FRAN             (*moving to* TIFFANY) Don't worry, West and I
                 will give you a hand. You must be Jennings?

| | |
|---|---|
| TIFFANY | Yeah, *Tiffany* Jennings ... that's me. |
| FRAN | (*shaking hands with* TIFFANY) I'm Jeffries. Do you have a handicap? |
| TIFFANY | Just Nick. |
| FRAN | Of the golfing variety? |
| TIFFANY | No. Can't see the point in golf really. |
| BARRY | Some people say it just spoils a good walk. (*Glum.*) Last round *I* had, it spoilt it a hundred and fourteen times. |
| TIFFANY | I don't like walking either. |
| NICK | *She* thinks walking spoils a good shop. |
| FRAN | (*to* TIFFANY) Nonsense. You can come out with me some time ... we'll soon have you hooked. (*To* BARRY.) Come along, West ... let's get these boxes out of the car. (*To* TIFFANY.) Keys? |
| TIFFANY | I left it open. |
| NICK | (*horrified.*) You did what? My clubs are in there! |
| TIFFANY | (*wearily*) It's alright, Nick ... I'm not stupid. The young kid said he'd keep an eye on them for me. |
| NICK | What kid? |
| TIFFANY | I don't know. He said he was a ball boy or something. |
| FRAN | (*urgently*) Don't worry, we're on our way. |

(FRAN *beckons* BARRY *to follow her and they exit to the car park.*)

NICK        Do you realise how much those clubs are worth?

SIMON       (*standing*) Of course, the club can't be held responsible for the theft of unattended equipment.

(SIMON *looks smugly at* NICK *but suddenly jumps in surprise, with a startled, wide-eyed expression on his face. It takes a second to register what is happening before he grabs at the outside of his trouser pocket, feeling for his phone.*)

NICK        Alright, mate?

SIMON       Yes ... not used to vibrate mode.

TIFFANY     (*pulling a face*) Bet that's your wife again.

NICK        Down his trouser leg?

(SIMON *reaches into his pocket and apologetically pulls the phone out of his pocket.*)

SIMON       (*blustering*) Probably official business ... Association of Golf Club Secretaries.

(SIMON *glances down at the phone to see who the caller is and he visibly wilts*) Ah ... (*He furtively edges away to one side, turning his back on* NICK *and* TIFFANY *for the duration of the call.*)

(*speaking into the phone as he turns*) Yes, my love? ...

TIFFANY     They've got a leak.

NICK        Yeah, well Simon's been wet for years.

TIFFANY     That Fran seems a bit funny as well. Why
            is she all, like, Armitage this and Jennings
            that?

NICK        Army.

TIFFANY     What?

NICK        She's in the army. Major Jeffries. She's
            the cutting edge of our front-line defence
            force ... as long as we don't get attacked on
            a weekend ... apparently the army doesn't
            do weekends anymore. (*Suddenly having
            a mischievous thought and, unseen by*
            TIFFANY, *smiling to himself. Confidentially.*)
            To be honest, her appointment was a bit
            controversial.

TIFFANY     How'd you mean?

NICK        Well, there was a bit of a conundr-i-um
            about whether she strictly qualified for
            being the *ladies* captain. Simon had to
            contact the Royal and Ancient for an
            official ruling.

TIFFANY     I'm still not with you.

NICK        (*sighing heavily*) Do I have to spell *everything*
            out? Let's just say that she used to be called
            Major *Frank* Jeffries.

TIFFANY     (*horrified and fascinated*) She never!

NICK        He did ... he did! Caused a lot of confusion
            on the parade ground ... his men never

knew whether he was going to salute or
curtsy. But look, eh, just keep it between
us, alright? There's only a few of us know
and we don't want to upset the other ladies.
Simon's worried that they might object to
her using the ladies facilities ... you see
... (*Wriggling his hips provocatively and
making a slicing motion with his hand.*) ...
we're not sure whether she's had the full
monty yet.

(BARRY *enters hurriedly and breathless
from the car park.*)

BARRY       They've gone!

NICK        Well, we don't know that. (*Suddenly
            registering that it's* BARRY.) What have?

BARRY       Your clubs.

TIFFANY     Oops!

BARRY       Sorry, Nick, we did our best but he
            disappeared faster than free beer at a
            Scotsman's funeral. Fran's gone chasing
            after him but I couldn't keep up.

NICK        Why didn't you jump in your car?

BARRY       (*sitting, trying to regain his breath*) That's a
            good point ... I never thought of that.

            (NICK *thinks quickly and moves hurriedly to*
            SIMON *and grabs his mobile from him.*)

SIMON       What are you doing?

| | |
|---|---|
| NICK | (*lifting the phone to his ear and speaking*) Sorry, Simon's got to go. He'll call you back … if you're unlucky.<br><br>(NICK *presses a key to ring off and then presses further keys to ring a number.*) |
| SIMON | You can't do that! It was an important call! |
| NICK | (*exiting to the car park*) I won't be long. |
| SIMON | (*outraged, to* BARRY *and* TIFFANY) He can't *do* that. (*Shouting after* NICK.) It's not on, Nicholas. |
| BARRY | I think he's ringing the police. |
| TIFFANY | His golf clubs have gone. He's going to kill me! |
| SIMON | Clubs? (*Distracted.*) Oh, right. (*Sighing and putting his hands up to his face and then shaking his head.*) I can't believe it. |
| TIFFANY | Something wrong? |
| SIMON | Yes … well that was my wife. |
| TIFFANY | (*pulling a sympathetic face*) Still flooded in your downstairs? |
| SIMON | Worse than that I'm afraid. |
| TIFFANY | Upstairs? It must be ever so deep. |
| SIMON | (*almost in shock*) She's just had a call from my mother, who seems to think she's having a heart attack. She's got funny pains. Well, probably not *funny* as such. Sounds quite serious. |

| TIFFANY | Oh, my God, that's awful! Is there anything we can do? |
|---------|-------------------------------------------------------|

| SIMON | No ... no ... it's all under control. Laura's given her a couple of aspirin and is driving her straight to hospital. |
|-------|------|

| BARRY | (*frowning*) Is that wise? |
|-------|------|

| SIMON | (*reflective*) Good point, Barry ... Laura's driving can be frightening for passengers at the best of times. |
|-------|------|

| BARRY | No, I meant get an ambulance. Mind you there's probably a three week waiting list. |
|-------|------|

| SIMON | No, I'm sure Laura knows best ... (*Gloomily.*) Laura *always* knows best. (*Pulling himself together.*) I appreciate your concern, both of you, but I'll be fine. |
|-------|------|

| TIFFANY | We'll keep our fingers crossed. |
|---------|------|

| SIMON | Thing is ... (*Shaking his head sadly.*) ... it's just so bloomin' inconvenient ... today of all days. |
|-------|------|

(*Lights fade.*)


Scene Two


*Mid day, the same day.* NICK's *folding 'halfway house' table has been covered with a white cloth and set up on, or partly on, the putting green. On it rests a two ring portable gas camping stove. On one of the rings is a kettle and on the other is a frying pan. One of the other patio tables has been moved near to it and the two tables are loaded with bread rolls, pies and soft drinks, etc.* TIFFANY *is wearing an apron and is standing behind the table, barefooted,*

*prodding hopefully at some sausages in the frying pan with
an expression on her face that clearly suggests that she has
no idea whatsoever what she is doing. She is using one of
the putting green flags as a make-shift spatula.* SIMON *exits
from the clubhouse bar, clearly pre-occupied. He stops
dead in his tracks, when he sees* TIFFANY *on the putting
green.*

| | |
|---|---|
| SIMON | (*horrified*) What are you doing? |
| TIFFANY | Sausages … (*Wrinkling her nose.*) … do they look done to you? |
| SIMON | I didn't mean *what* are you doing … I mean what are you *doing*? |
| TIFFANY | (*frowning*) Still sausages. |
| SIMON | You're on the bloomin' putting green, woman! |
| TIFFANY | (*cheerfully*) Yeah … I thought it made it look nice and picnicky. |
| SIMON | Do you realise how much effort goes into getting it in such pristine condition? |
| TIFFANY | Looked a bit scabby to me. Anyway, sorry, but it's full of holes. |
| SIMON | (*condescending*) Those are for the members to practice putting into. That's why it's called a putting green. |
| TIFFANY | No, not the *big* holes, silly … I mean the *little* holes. (*Reaching down to pick up one of her shoes and holding it up for* SIMON *to see. Guiltily.*) I was sinking in a bit. |
| SIMON | (*moving to examine the green*) Oh, my God! |

TIFFANY        (*pulling a face*) Yeah, wherever I stood it
               was like ... oops! (*Brightly.*) But it's alright
               ... I've taken them off now.

SIMON          (*shaking his head*) Haven't any of the
               members told you to move?

TIFFANY        Oh, a few have ... but I just told them to
               bog off.

               (SIMON *looks aghast.*)

               Only kidding. I just told them that you said
               it was alright.

SIMON          What? That's even worse!

TIFFANY        Well, you never said it *wasn't* alright and
               there was nobody here to ask!

SIMON          (*straightening chairs, agitated*) Do you
               realise how this is going to make me look in
               front of the Greens Committee? It's a fiasco
               ... it's just not on! (*With a sudden thought.*)
               Have you got a food hygiene certificate?

TIFFANY        (*looking around helplessly at the chaos
               surrounding her*) Do I *look* like I've got a
               food hygiene certificate?

SIMON          Mmm ... point taken. Message received
               and understood. But what if you poison
               everyone? How's that going to make *me*
               look?

TIFFANY        (*giggling*) Like an accomplice I suppose.

               (*The sound of a ball being driven off a
               nearby tee is heard.*)

SIMON          (*looking out on to the golf course and
               shouting*) That's the way, Roger, nice and
               steady.

               (SIMON *mimes a golf swing but gets a twinge
               in his back and winces as he rubs at it.*)

TIFFANY        (*sympathetic*) Any news of your poor
               mother?

SIMON          (*holding the back of a chair and stretching
               his back awkwardly*) No, nothing as yet.

TIFFANY        Well, no news is good news I suppose ...
               I heard straight away when my Gran died
               after her chain saw accident. It nearly made
               me go veggie 'cos it turns my stomach
               going in the butchers now. Anyway, I expect
               you'll get an update very soon because the
               most amazing ...

               (TIFFANY *is distracted as* NICK, BARRY *and*
               FRAN *enter from the golf course.* NICK *is
               now wearing garish golfing clothes and
               wears a baseball cap back to front.* BARRY'S
               *shirt is completely untucked. They are all
               clearly in the middle of their round of golf
               and carrying score cards and pencils.*)

NICK           And I'm telling you it was only a five.

FRAN           Nonsense, two penalty strokes. You were
               clearly trying to improve your lie.

NICK           No I wasn't! I was only jumping up and
               down because ... well, I was being attacked
               by a dirty great wasp.

TIFFANY        Is he cheating again? Barry says he's always
               cheating.

(SIMON *spots* BARRY'S *shirt and points at him, indicating that he tuck it in, which* BARRY *reluctantly does.*)

BARRY It's more a liberal interpretation of the rules ... which is alright when he's on my side like he is today.

FRAN (*sitting*) Nonsense, I'm marking it down as a seven.

(FRAN *fills in a scorecard. The sound of a ball being driven off a nearby tee is heard. It is followed by a loud cry of "Fore left". They all duck and cover their heads with the exception of* TIFFANY *who watches them all in bewilderment. The sound of a breaking clubhouse window is heard, off.* SIMON *takes his notebook from his pocket as he glares out front to see who was responsible.*)

NICK (*giving a 'thumbs-up' and shouting, out front*) Nice one, Bill ... still got the hook.

SIMON (*mumbling to himself as he writes in the notebook*) Warning letter to William ...

TIFFANY Are you meant to do that?

NICK Of course you're not meant to ... (*Suddenly realises that* TIFFANY *has set things up on the putting green and moving to her.*) Tiffany! What are you doing?

TIFFANY Sausages.

SIMON (*putting the notebook back in his pocket*) We've already been through all that! Why did you let her set up on there?

NICK            (*ignoring* SIMON *and moving to* TIFFANY)
                Are you simple or something? You'll get me
                excommunicated.

TIFFANY         It's not my fault! If you'd helped before
                you wandered off to play your silly game it
                wouldn't have been a problem. I don't know
                all the stupid rules.

SIMON           I'll be making out a full report on the
                matter, Nicholas. I'm sure you'll be called
                upon to explain why your guest wilfully
                despoiled the practice putting surface.
                (*Pointedly turning* NICK'S *cap the right way
                round*.) I shouldn't be surprised if a lengthy
                period of suspension isn't imposed.

NICK            (*threatening and pointedly turning his cap
                the wrong way round again*) And *I* shouldn't
                be surprised if my seven iron doesn't get
                lodged in your skull!

FRAN            Gentlemen, this is no time for bickering.

                (*The sound of a ball being driven off a
                nearby tee is heard, followed by the same
                voice shouting "Fore right". They all
                ignore it with the exception of* TIFFANY *who
                shrieks and ducks down behind the table.
                They all turn to look at her in disbelief as
                she sheepishly rises from behind the table*.)

                As it happens the woeful condition of the
                putting green was one of the other points
                my ladies wanted to raise. (*Moving to*
                TIFFANY.) I forbid you to move, Jennings, the
                whole thing needs relaying.

SIMON           The Head Green Keeper won't be happy.

BARRY

The Head Green Keeper's never happy. He hates people using his course. I wouldn't like to be in your shoes.

SIMON

My shoes? (*Pointing indignantly.*) It's *her* shoes that have made all the bloomin' holes!

BARRY

But you told me he'd charged you with the organisation of the practice putting green. It doesn't look very well organised to me.

SIMON

(*defeated*) No ... point taken ... point taken, Barry.

(SIMON *looks worried and thoughtful for a moment before having a flash of inspiration, pulling a large bunch of keys from his pocket and looking through them thoughtfully.*)

Still, not much harm done. Soon fix that. (*Pause.*) Good. Back in a jiff.

(SIMON *suddenly dashes off to the Green Keeper's compound, leaving the others staring after him in surprised silence.*)

FRAN

(*breaking the silence*) Odd sort of chap.

NICK

(*sitting*) Always has been ... although to be honest, he's a bit of a star really. I mean, who else would want to be Secretary?

BARRY

That's true. I don't thing we've got any other self-obsessed, fascist megalomaniacs in the club.

FRAN

Actually, you've probably just described half of the club membership.

(*The others nod in silent agreement.* NICK *turns his cap the correct way round and starts to study his scorecard*)

(*to* TIFFANY) So, what have you got for us, Jennings?

TIFFANY           Tiffany.

FRAN              Sorry, Tiffany ... force of habit.

(TIFFANY *is clearly intrigued by the story that* NICK *has told her about* FRAN. *Throughout the following dialogue, she is distracted as she tries to assess* FRAN. *The more* TIFFANY *tries to be casual, the more obvious it becomes that she is fascinated by* FRAN'S *appearance.*)

TIFFANY           What have I got? ... Oh ... well, (*Making a conscious effort to use her 'air hostess voice' and using her hands and arms to demonstrate the position of the various items.*) I have hot sausage sandwiches, steak and kidney pies, and for the vegetarian option I have ... I have ...

(TIFFANY *tails off as she loses concentration and looks* FRAN *up and down.* FRAN *can't quite understand why* TIFFANY *is looking at her so closely.*)

FRAN              You have?

TIFFANY           (*pulling herself together and giggling nervously*) For the vegetarian option I have a small selection of delicious sandwiches. Only it's not really a selection because there's only one sort ... (*Mentally wandering off as she looks at* FRAN *again,*

> *then pulling herself back together.*) ... and it's not really vegetarian either. That's Nick's fault.

NICK            (*with total conviction*) Of course it's veggie!

TIFFANY         (*in her normal voice*) Nick, it's tuna. Tunas aren't veggie.

NICK            Course they are ... they haven't got feet have they?

> (TIFFANY's *gaze returns to* FRAN *and she looks her up and down, smiling vacantly. She suddenly realises that* FRAN *is watching her, puzzled.*)

TIFFANY         (*trying to continue professionally in her 'air hostess voice'*) And finally, I have a comprehensive range of hot (*Miming wiping sweat from her brow.*) and cold (*Rubbing her hands together.*) beverages, including tea (*Lifting the kettle and touching it with a finger.*) ... ouch! (*Flinching and putting the kettle down hurriedly.*) ... coffee and orange squash ... (*Frowning.*) in fact that's all there is, so it's more minimal than comprehensive.

> (TIFFANY *smiles at* FRAN *and there is an embarrassed silence as they look at each other.* FRAN *is totally bemused.*)

> (*feeling that she should say something but reverting to her normal voice*) The doctor said that when the swelling went down he'd probably be able to walk again, but I'm afraid the boy said that he was going to sue you.

FRAN        What?

TIFFANY     When I took him to Casualty. He seemed
            quite switched on. He said that you'd
            infringed his human rights by depriving
            him of the opportunity to play golf.

NICK        But he'd stolen *my* clubs.

TIFFANY     Don't think that matters these days, Nick.
            Oh, and he mentioned grievous bodily harm
            as well.

FRAN        It's all nonsense of course. I only gave him
            the lightest of cuffs ... hardly drew any
            blood at all.

TIFFANY     Just the twenty three stitches. (*Pulling a
            note from her apron pocket and passing it
            to* FRAN.) And the policeman said would you
            give him a ring about making a statement.

FRAN        Some 'jobsworth' I suppose. Anyway,
            thank you for taking the boy to hospital.
            Personally I'd have left him lying on the
            verge. (*Disconcerted by the way* TIFFANY *is
            looking at her.*) Are you alright?

TIFFANY     Yes, thank you. And yourself?

FRAN        Fine, yes.

TIFFANY     Good.

FRAN        (*to* NICK *and* BARRY) Right. You two chaps
            about ready to kick on?

BARRY       I was going to have a sarnie first! No point
            Tiffs going to all this trouble if we don't
            stop for a few minutes.

| | |
|---|---|
| FRAN | (*glancing at the note*) I'd better ring this chap then ... then I'll pay a quick visit and we'll be off. Steak pie for me ... plenty of brown sauce. |
| | (FRAN *strides off into the bar.*) |
| BARRY | (*peering over* TIFFANY'S *shoulder at the food*) Sausage sarnie for me, Tiffs. |
| NICK | I'd be careful if I were you, mate ... she's a crap cook. |
| TIFFANY | Nick! It's not my fault is it? (*Confidentially to* BARRY.) Which one does she normally use? |
| BARRY | Who? |
| TIFFANY | Fran. |
| BARRY | I don't know. HP I suppose. Can I have a well done one, please? |
| TIFFANY | I meant which toilet. (TIFFANY *pokes at the sausages as* BARRY *looks at her, mystified.* NICK *stifles a snigger.*) They're all a bit pink in the middle and they smell a bit funny. Is that alright? |
| BARRY | (*looking at the sausages with distaste*) Tell you what ... I'll have a pie. |
| TIFFANY | How's the game going? |
| BARRY | (*disconsolate*) Alright. |
| NICK | Barry's an honorary woman for the day ... there weren't enough to go round. |

BARRY
(*sulking*) It's humiliating, Tiffs, it really is. Nick's making me play off the ladies' tees.

NICK
(*scathing*) And it's just a pity that you're not taking advantage of it!

(SIMON *enters from the direction of the Green Keeper's compound, carrying a spade.*)

SIMON
(*tossing his keys onto one of the patio tables as he passes it*) Here we are. Good job I've got a key to the Green Keeper's compound. (*To* TIFFANY.) Excuse me.

(TIFFANY *moves to one side and* SIMON *starts tapping tentatively with the back of the spade at the surface of the putting green where she has been standing.*)

TIFFANY
Hey, you'll never guess who I bumped into at the hospital, Nick. It was quite weird really.

NICK
Erm … Elvis Presley?

TIFFANY
Simon's wife. (*To* SIMON.) We got on really well … she was quite chatty.

SIMON
(*standing bolt upright, suddenly alert*) What? My wife? But you don't know her.

TIFFANY
No, but when I was waiting in Casualty I sat next to a lady and we got talking. Then it dawned who she was. How spooky is that? (*Reassuring.*) Oh, I said that I thought you were a very nice man. She seemed quite interested that you were at the golf club.

SIMON
You didn't tell her?

TIFFANY          Yes ... (*Realizing.*) ... oops. Sorry.

SIMON            (*flustered, with a haunted look*) Right.
                 (*Propping the spade up against the end of
                 the table and feeling in his pocket.*) Car
                 keys ... where did I put my car keys.

NICK             (*enjoying* SIMON'S *discomfort*) Dashing off?

SIMON            Yes. Other pressing engagements.
                 (*Confidentially.*) Look, if anybody asks, I
                 haven't been here today ... it was just a mix
                 up ... a mistake. Alright?

NICK             You mean you want us to lie to Laura?

SIMON            Good Lord, no ... no, I wouldn't want that.
                 Well ... yes ... just as chums ... I mean
                 we're all chums aren't we? (*Turning* NICK'S
                 *cap the wrong way around.*) Might have our
                 differences but that's only natural. Barry?

BARRY            But about a hundred people must have seen
                 you already. They can't all be chums can
                 they?

SIMON            (*frowning*) No ... in fact some of them can
                 be quite off-hand ... I'd have them out.
                 (*Thinking hard.*) Ah ... but ... they may
                 well have seen someone who *looked* like
                 me ... (*Touching his nose.*) some kind of
                 doppelganger perhaps. (*Looking up and
                 seeing* LAURA *approaching.*) Oh, no!

                 (SIMON *looks around, searching for an
                 escape route, but realises that it is too late.
                 * LAURA *enters from the car park. She is
                 well groomed and wearing a smart summer
                 dress. As she spots* SIMON *her expression
                 becomes thunderous.*)

| | |
|---|---|
| NICK | (*gleeful at* SIMON'S *obvious discomfort*) Oh, yes. |
| LAURA | So you *are* here. |
| SIMON | (*weakly*) Not really, my love ... no. |
| NICK | (*cheerily*) Morning, Laura. You alright? |
| LAURA | Good morning, Nick ... (*Looking around she sees* BARRY *and her expression softens, almost imperceptibly.*) ... Barry. |
| | (BARRY *looks slightly startled and embarrassed to see* LAURA *and he simply smiles weakly back at her.*) |
| NICK | I believe you've met Tiffs? |
| LAURA | (*glancing at* TIFFANY) Yes, hello Tiffany ... we meet again. |
| TIFFANY | (*embarrassed*) Yes ... we do ... (*Pulling a face and pointing vaguely at* SIMON.) ... oops! |
| LAURA | Oops indeed! |
| NICK | I suppose you're looking for Simon? |
| LAURA | I can't think why I would bother, but yes. |
| NICK | (*enjoying himself enormously*) Unfortunately he's not here. Sadly missed of course. |
| | (LAURA *looks at* NICK *as though he is an idiot and then looks questioningly at* SIMON.) |

Oh, no, no, no ... that's not him. He's just one of our other golfing ... (*Pointedly turning his cap the right way round as he grins at* SIMON.) ... chums, was it?

TIFFANY        (*helpfully*) Mister Dopple.

LAURA          Dopple?

SIMON          Ganger. I was just having a joke with them.

LAURA          You never joke with anyone, Simon. You wouldn't know how to.

SIMON          Not true actually, my love ... nobody enjoys a good chuckle more than me. (*Conversationally.*) How's mother?

LAURA          How's mother? You mean *your* mother? The one who *I* have had to take to hospital because *you* were too busy in a fictitious meeting with some fictitious client?

SIMON          Oh no, not fictitious ... just unbelievably short.

LAURA          The meeting or the client?

SIMON          (*laughing very falsely*) Very good, Laura ... very funny. I've just got here ... apparently I have a crisis to resolve ... haven't I, Nicholas?

NICK           You have *now*, yeah.

LAURA          So you've just arrived?

SIMON          Just this minute.

| | |
|---|---|
| LAURA | (*glancing at* TIFFANY) Strange that Tiffany should have seen you here earlier then. Sounds to me as though you've been here all morning. |
| SIMON | Well ... not *all* morning, obviously ... |
| NICK | It just *seems* like he's been here a long time ... you know what he's like. |
| LAURA | Sadly, I do ... yes. The club is obviously more important than the flooding of his house and the illness of his mother! |
| NICK | Ah well, I suppose all things are relative. |
| LAURA | Since you ask, Simon, your mother has now been admitted to hospital. The last report I had was that she's comfortable ... although she doesn't seem to agree with them. As I left she was complaining about everything from the lumpiness of the mattress to the fact that she didn't like the look of the other people on the ward. |
| SIMON | Well don't you think you should have stayed with her? |
| LAURA | Me? |
| SIMON | Well, you were the one with the hand on the tiller so to speak. I mean I'd never forgive myself if something happened and you'd left her on her own. |
| TIFFANY | I hope she'll be alright. I hate hospitals. (*Passing* BARRY *a pie.*) My gran went to two of them after her accident. |

LAURA                I doubt there'll be any need for Simon's
                     mother to be transferred. I suspect that it's
                     only indigestion.

                     (BARRY *takes a bite from his pie.*)

TIFFANY              Oh, she wasn't transferred. Two ambulances
                     turned up and there was a bit of a mix up.
                     Most of her went to the District hospital but
                     her leg went to the County. It was like ...
                     oops ... big mistake.

                     (BARRY *suddenly loses his appetite and
                     chews distastefully at the portion of pie
                     in his mouth. He looks at the contents of
                     the pie in his hand and hands it back to*
                     TIFFANY.)

                     (*Surprised.*) Don't you like it?

BARRY                (*swallowing with difficulty*) Lost my
                     appetite a bit.

SIMON                So it's just indigestion then?

LAURA                I don't know ... probably. You know what
                     your mother's like. The last time she had
                     a headache she tried to admit herself for a
                     brain scan.

SIMON                They wouldn't have found much! This
                     is typical of her ... absolutely bloomin'
                     typical. She's just trying to ruin my day. It's
                     all because I said I wouldn't go and cut her
                     lawn today ... she knew I had plans.

LAURA                Well, it's a pity you didn't see fit to tell *me*
                     about your plans!

(SIMON *notices that the others are listening and takes* LAURA'S *arm to pull her away to one of the tables for a more private conversation.*)

SIMON       The reason I didn't tell you about my plans is that when I *do* tell you about my plans you go off on one of your ... your rants. Alright? Point taken?

LAURA       Rants? You're saying that I rant? Well, the only reason that I *rant*, Simon, is because you're so bloody inconsiderate. Every weekend it's the same. "Just popping out, won't be long" ...

            (LAURA *and* SIMON *sit as they continue to argue. During the course of the following passage they eventually fall silent,* LAURA *fiddling with her mobile and* SIMON *watching her moodily.*)

TIFFANY     Are you having a sausage sarnie, Nick?

NICK        You must be joking. I'm not risking any of that stuff.

TIFFANY     It's not my fault I can't cook. You shouldn't have asked me to do it.

NICK        It's not your cooking I'm worried about. Just go in and get me a bar of chocolate or something.

TIFFANY     Why can't you get it yourself?

NICK        Because I'm in the middle of a golf game aren't I? I need to stay focussed. I'm a finely honed athlete.

(BARRY *sniggers*.)

TIFFANY        Well, you'll have to keep an eye on these. I
               don't know whether they're done or not.

               (TIFFANY *exits into the bar*.)

BARRY          Honed athlete?

NICK           Yes Barry. I've been working out. (*Trying
               to pull his stomach in*.) I've got quite a six
               pack now.

BARRY          Buy one get one free was it? (*Prodding at
               the sausages with a fork*.) What's wrong
               with these then? It's not like you to turn
               down high cholesterol junk food.

NICK           That, Barry, is not junk food. Nothing
               but the best for Jeff's big day. These are
               premium quality, hand crafted sausages and
               pies ... they're just a bit past their use-by
               date. Couldn't knock the price though.

BARRY          How much were they?

NICK           Nothing. I picked 'em up at the pub last
               week ... the chef was slinging 'em in the
               skip.

BARRY          What?

NICK           Anyway, you've got enough to think about
               without worrying about the food.

BARRY          Like what?

NICK           Your game. You're going to have to pull
               your finger out if we're going to win. What
               you need, Barry, me old mate, me old

mucker, (*Ostentatiously miming a drive*.) is a better driver.

BARRY       But I've only just got a new one. It's a bit disappointing really 'cos I thought it would make all the difference.

NICK        But you bought cheap didn't you? I warned you. Luckily for you I have my old one in the locker ... seventy quid and it's yours.

BARRY       I can't change in the middle of a round ... it's against the rules!

NICK        It's Captain's Day, Bas. I'm the acting captain and I give you permission. Cash up front mind.

            (NICK *moves to exit into the changing rooms*.)

BARRY       But I'm not sure I want to change.

NICK        Rubbish. Trust me. Swap the head covers round and nobody will notice.

            (NICK *exits, leaving* BARRY *prodding thoughtfully at the food.* LAURA *looks round at* SIMON *as she puts her mobile back in her bag*.)

LAURA       You still here? Isn't it time you got off.

SIMON       Got off where?

LAURA       Your mother's expecting you.

SIMON       But I'm needed here! I thought you could go back and sit with her. Nice gesture. She'd appreciate it.

LAURA      Oh no, you're not passing this one off on
           me. I've done my bit. She's *your* mother.

SIMON      (*reflective*) Fair enough. Good point. You're
           right, I'm just being selfish. Best leave
           her in peace ... give her chance to rest. I
           mean you've done all you can ... enough
           said ... much appreciated. They'll give her
           a cardiograph and send her home with a
           couple of indigestion tablets. She'll enjoy
           the ambulance ride.

LAURA      But what if something happens, Simon?

SIMON      No, I know my mother. I know her plan.
           Absolutely par for the course. Maximum
           attention for herself ... maximum disruption
           to everybody else. Well she's not doing it
           ... not today ... not to you. Shouldn't you be
           getting back for the plumber?

LAURA      No I should not! Why should I sit at home
           with no water while you lord it over
           everyone here? No, he's gone off to get
           some parts and I gave him a key.

SIMON      A key? Is he trustworthy?

LAURA      He said he was a member *here* so I rather
           doubt it. Nevertheless, I am going to stay
           right here and have a drink. Gin and tonic
           please.

SIMON      Gin? Bit early isn't it?

LAURA      I've had two hours with your mother.

| | |
|---|---|
| SIMON | Point taken. Message received and understood. (*Sniffing reluctantly.*) Seeing as you're here. |
| | (SIMON *exits into the bar. As he passes* BARRY.) Shirt, Barry. |
| | (LAURA *looks over towards* BARRY. *He senses her looking at him and tries to avoid eye contact with her.* LAURA *moves towards* BARRY, *who looks uncomfortable as she approaches.*) |
| LAURA | Quite the chef. |
| BARRY | Who, me? Not really, no. I'm just ... well, you know me ... seem to get landed with everything. |
| LAURA | Tell me about it. |
| BARRY | Tiffs'll be back in a minute and then I'll ... you know ... (*Swinging an imaginary golf club.*) |
| LAURA | Chop a tree down? |
| BARRY | Is my swing that bad? |
| | (*There is a rather uncomfortable silence.* LAURA *glances into the bar to make sure they can't be overheard before turning back to* BARRY.) |
| BARRY | I don't think I ... |
| | (*together*) |
| LAURA | So is that what ... |
| BARRY | Sorry. |

LAURA      Is that what you think of *me* then?

BARRY      I don't know what you mean?

LAURA      Something that you got *landed* with? An unpleasant little interlude between golf rounds?

BARRY      No, of course not. It wasn't like that at all.

LAURA      So why have you been avoiding me?

BARRY      Because I thought that was what we agreed. (*There is an uneasy pause.*) Do you want a sausage?

LAURA      Not really.

BARRY      Wise decision.

LAURA      Do you realise that we haven't actually seen each other since the Valentine's Day Dinner?

BARRY      Which was a bit of a disaster as I recollect. A furtive grope behind the Green Keeper's tool shed and then back for the last dance with hubby.

LAURA      You must have got it wrong ... I don't do furtive gropes.

BARRY      Must have been a different woman then. Whichever one it was told me, if I remember correctly, that she didn't want to see me any more.

LAURA      I didn't say that ... I said I *shouldn't* see you any more.

| | |
|---|---|
| BARRY | So why have you been sending me endless text messages and tried phoning me at improbable hours? |
| LAURA | All of which you've ignored. |
| BARRY | I didn't ignore the texts ... I read them all. |
| LAURA | And? |
| BARRY | And I don't really think you're being very fair. |
| LAURA | In what way? |
| BARRY | Look, let's just leave it. |
| LAURA | No, I *won't* leave it. |
| BARRY | Alright then. It's not fair that you expect me to be at your beck and call every time you happen to fall out with Simon. Alright? It's not fair on me and I don't think it's very fair on Simon actually. |
| LAURA | Simon doesn't have a concept of fair ... he only has a concept of what's good for Simon. You're a lifeline, Barry! I need you. |
| BARRY | Me or anybody else who happens to be around? |
| LAURA | (*hurt*) Now who's not being fair? |
| BARRY | And what if Simon found out. |
| LAURA | Simon? He's so busy shuffling his precious bloody diary about ... (*Emphasising her point with gestured quotation marks.*) "Critical Golfing Events" and "Crucial |

Business Scenarios" ... that he wouldn't actually notice if you came round to the house and we had it off on his remote control leather recliner. Of course, if there was a golf match on the television he'd probably ask us to move to the settee.

BARRY          No change since you moved house then?

LAURA          I was stupid to think there would be. A project we could both get involved in ... something to share. The only change is that I now have a constant stream of tradesmen turning up to do all the jobs *he* ignores. If I have to make one more cup of bloody builders tea ...! (*Moving close to* BARRY *and putting a hand on his arm*.) We need to talk.

               (BARRY *is uncomfortable with* LAURA's *close proximity in a public place. He looks up to see whether anybody is watching and sees somebody he recognises. He moves slightly away from* LAURA *and waves out front*.)

BARRY          (*shouting*) Now then, Mike, how's it going? ... Sausage sarnie when you've putted out?

               (TIFFANY *and* SIMON *enter together from the bar. She is carrying a chocolate bar and* SIMON *is carrying a gin and tonic. When* LAURA *sees them she moves away from* BARRY.)

TIFFANY        (*confidentially to* SIMON) I don't think there's anything to worry about.

SIMON          In what respect?

TIFFANY     The *lady* captain. I followed her into the
            ladies and everything seemed to be ... you
            know ... as expected.

SIMON       What?

TIFFANY     She definitely didn't put the seat up 'cos I
            was listening.

SIMON       (*totally mystified*) Good ... good. Well
            done. Excellent. Point taken.

            (TIFFANY *moves to* BARRY *and organises
            things on the table.* SIMON *moves to* LAURA
            *and gives her the drink.*)

            One gin and tonic. On reflection, I still
            think it's a bit early ... we don't want any
            scenes ... not here. (*Looking out front,
            waving and shouting.*) Oh, nice putt,
            Michael ... oh, hard luck, just lipped out ...
            I thought it was in.

LAURA       (*through gritted teeth*) And what does that
            mean?

SIMON       (*distracted by watching*) What? ... Oh, his
            ball caught the edge of the hole and shot
            round it. It's called lipping out. Technical
            term ... no need to worry yourself. (*With an
            expansive gesture.*) Bit like sling-shotting
            around the moon.

LAURA       I mean what kind of scene?

SIMON       Scene? (*Suddenly switching his attention
            back to* LAURA.) Well, you know ... when
            you've had a drink you can get a bit ... edgy
            ... tetchy. Yes, that's a good word for it ...
            tetchy. Enough said? Point taken?

LAURA        No ... the point isn't bloody well taken. Are
             you saying I can't take a drink?

SIMON        No, I'm not saying that at all. To be fair,
             you can probably take it better than most
             ... I mean you get plenty of practice when
             all's said and done. All I'm saying is that ...
             (*Suddenly distracted as he looks out on to
             the course.*) ... oh hang on, there's Smithy, I
             need a word.

             (SIMON *moves to exit toward the imagined
             'Smithy'.*)

LAURA        (*shouting*) Simon!

SIMON        (*turning back, alarmed*) Ssshhhh ...
             (*Moving back to* LAURA.) ... there are people
             putting out.

LAURA        Simon, I don't care if there are people
             putting out, putting up or putting their
             bloody putters somewhere where the sun
             doesn't shine! We are in the middle of a
             conversation ... or perhaps more accurately
             an argument!

SIMON        There you are you see ... there you go. All
             I did was take the trouble to point out one
             teeny, little fault and you accuse me of
             arguing! All I'm saying is that one drink is
             probably enough. I mean, I'm not even sure
             that it's quite appropriate ... I can't afford
             to have people talking.

LAURA        Appropriate?

SIMON        With my mother lying in hospital at death's
             door ... and here you are knocking it back
             as though you haven't got a care in the

world! Enough said? Now, if you don't mind, Laura, it's absolutely *critical* that I have a word with Smithy about the new club tie motifs. Fair enough? Alright?

(LAURA *quietly seethes as* SIMON *exits purposefully.*)

LAURA

(*shouting after him*) Best get them done in black for your mother's bloody funeral!

(LAURA *looks back out front and realises that she has just spoilt somebody's putt.*)

(*raising her hand apologetically and calling out front*) Sorry … sorry. It's just that he's a bit of a pillock … sorry.

(LAURA *moves to a table and sits.*)

TIFFANY

(*to* BARRY) Oops. I'll just be a minute.

BARRY

Fine … fine … nothing better to do.

(TIFFANY *moves to* LAURA *and sits down next to her. During the following conversation,* LAURA *occasionally glances out, watching* SIMON *in the distance.*)

TIFFANY

I couldn't help overhearing. I'm terribly sorry.

LAURA

About Simon being a pillock? Don't be … he's always been a pillock … as were his father and grandfather before him.

TIFFANY

No, I mean his mother.

LAURA

Oh. Well that side of his family's rather different. They tend to specialise in lunacy.

Unfortunately, Simon's inherited the full
defective gene bank from both sides.

TIFFANY      (*unsure how to react*) But even so ... I know
             she was in hospital but it's still a bit of a
             shock.

             (LAURA *looks at her blankly*.)

             The funeral. (*Trying hard to be
             sympathetic*.) Will you go for burial or
             cremation?

LAURA        To be honest I'd be happy either way.

TIFFANY      I prefer cremation 'cos I think it's probably
             greener ... although I suppose you do get a
             lot of smoke which can't be very good for
             your carbon footprint. Don't suppose you
             care about that when you're dead though.
             We had my gran cremated ... well, most of
             her. It was quite nice ... I cried.

LAURA        Yes, cremation would be nice. I'd rush the
             arrangements through but, sadly, I fear
             we're going to have to hang on until she's
             actually dead.

TIFFANY      You mean she isn't?

LAURA        I'm sure we'd have heard.

TIFFANY      Oops. Sorry.

             (TIFFANY *and* LAURA *sit in silence as* FRAN
             *enters from the bar. She moves to* BARRY.
             TIFFANY *watches her with interest*.)

FRAN          All ready, West? You and Armitage are
              going to have to buck your ideas up if you
              want to beat us.

BARRY         I don't think my partner's too pleased with
              my performance so far.

FRAN          Nonsense. Just forget about your fourteen
              on the eighth ... it's a tricky bunker.

BARRY         I spent longer in the sand than Lawrence of
              Arabia!

FRAN          Chin up, arm straight ... you'll be fine.

BARRY         Oh, I've tried all that. If I swing like the
              pro tells me, I feel like an octopus falling
              out of a tree.

FRAN          Mmm. Perhaps your talents lie in other
              areas.

BARRY         I shouldn't think so. I've tried every sport
              known to man. I used to fancy myself at
              tenpin bowling before the accident.

              (FRAN *looks at him quizzically.*)

              I was a tad over-enthusiastic and got to the
              pins before the ball. Three hundred quids
              worth of damage and concussion. I got
              banned.

FRAN          I was thinking more of an admin-type role.
              The club always needs good committee
              men. I'm on the House Committee and they
              need a damn good shake up.

BARRY         Oh, I'm not sure about ...

FRAN          Good ... that's settled then. You know, I
              think you and I would make a pretty good
              combination. (*Hesitantly, but affectionately
              punching* BARRY's *arm.*) We should have a
              few drinks together sometime ... what do
              you say?

BARRY         Well, I don't know.

FRAN          Excellent. That's a date. My pie ready?

BARRY         I wouldn't if I were you. They're a bit
              suspect.

              (BARRY *picks one of the pies up and bangs
              it on the edge of the table. It makes a solid
              wooden sound.*)

FRAN          (*taking the pie from* BARRY) I've had worse.

              (NICK *enters breezily.*)

NICK          Right, are we ready?

FRAN          Ready? My partner's been champing at the
              bit on the tee for the last ten minutes!

NICK          Well that's not my fault is it. To be honest,
              we could have got going ages ago if Gordon
              Ramsey here had got his act together. (*To*
              BARRY.) I've stuck it in your bag. One hit
              and you owe me eighty quid mind.

BARRY         You said seventy.

NICK          Yes, well, I was doing myself ... it's like
              new.

FRAN          What's all this?

NICK        Never you mind ... team tactics. Tiffany,
            get yourself over here ... celebrity master
            chef here has 'ready steady cooked' himself
            out. (*Pointing out front.*) And that lot'll
            be off the green wanting subsidence in a
            minute ... if any of them can manage to get
            the flipping ball in the hole.

TIFFANY     Yeah, I'm coming.

            (TIFFANY *moves to* NICK *and gives him the
            chocolate bar.*)

NICK        Here, Tiffs ... here. Just you get them all
            to sign a disclaim-i-er before they bite into
            anything. Can you cope?

TIFFANY     Looks like I'll have to. Enjoy the rest of
            your silly game.

NICK        (*giving* TIFFANY *a quick kiss, then pointing
            at* BARRY) That all depends on wonder
            woman here pulling his finger out and
            giving me a bit of support.

FRAN        (*putting her arm round* BARRY *and leading
            him off onto the course*) Take no notice of
            him, West. You just carry on as you were.

NICK        (*following them off*) That's what I'm
            worried about. You don't want him on a free
            transfer do you?

            (TIFFANY *watches them leave, still
            fascinated by* FRAN.)

TIFFANY     (*calling across to* LAURA) You'd never guess
            would you?

(LAURA *is lost in her own thoughts and stares moodily out to the front, not realizing that* TIFFANY *is talking to her.*)

(*To herself.*) Well, *I'd* never guess.

(SIMON *enters hurriedly from the course. He off-handedly acknowledges* TIFFANY *with a slight wave of the hand but walks past* LAURA *without appearing to notice her. He is about to enter the bar.*)

LAURA      (*sarcastically*) Hello, Laura ... oh, hello, Simon ... nice to see you ... would you like anything else?

SIMON      (*turning*) What?

LAURA      Oh nothing, just chatting to myself. Thought I'd gone invisible.

SIMON      (*moving back to her*) Why, what's wrong?

LAURA      Nothing's wrong, Simon. I love sitting here in splendid, solitary isolation, with you ignoring me.

SIMON      I'm not ignoring you. It's just that I'm very busy.

LAURA      Yes, of course, darling. Silly old me.

SIMON      (*patiently*) Laura, have you any idea of the burden of responsibility that rests on my shoulders as Club Secretary? I'm the nerve centre.

LAURA      You're certainly getting on *my* nerves.

| | |
|---|---|
| SIMON | People rely on me ... people expect me to be available at a moment's notice ... some of them can barely tie their own shoelaces. |
| LAURA | From what I've seen, most people see you coming and immediately scuttle off as fast as their legs can carry them! You must have chased that 'Smiffy' for fifty yards. |
| SIMON | Yes, well, he's let me down. You'll never guess what he's done? Go on, I'll give you three guesses ... go on. |
| LAURA | Erm ... ooh ... that's a hard one. I mean, we all let you down don't we? Erm ... oh, I know ... he slighty overdid your boiled egg this morning and made your little toasty soldier snap in half? Oh no, silly ... that was me wasn't it? I give in. |
| SIMON | Very funny. He's only gone and messed up the new club ties, hasn't he. I was at pains to specify that we required the fifty eight inch, and he's only gone and ordered the bloomin' fifty four inch. |
| LAURA | (*in mock horror*) Oh, God, no! |
| SIMON | Oh yes, it's all very well for *you* to mock but it's me who's got to clear up the mess. I mean, they might be acceptable to the shorter members but what about the taller ones ... they're going to end up looking like Laurel and Hardy! |
| LAURA | From what I've seen, most of them play golf like Laurel and Hardy. |
| SIMON | (*looking at his watch*) Right. (*Checking things off in his notebook.*) Ties ... |

tick. Revised handicap sheets ... tick.
Replacement cruet sets ... tick. Anything
else? (*Decisive.*) Right, I'm off. I expect
you'll be gone when I get back.

LAURA            (*surprised*) Oh, so you *are* going?

SIMON            Yes, of course. I might not like it but I've
                 always known where my duty lies, Laura,
                 you can't deny that.

LAURA            Oh well ... (*Softening, and quickly finishing
                 her drink.*) ... I'll come with you ... I
                 suppose I'd better show some interest.

SIMON            You?

LAURA            Yes, why not?

SIMON            You've never shown any interest before.
                 You're not really dressed for it.

LAURA            It's only a hospital, Simon, it's not Royal
                 Ascot.

SIMON            Hospital? No, I'm expected on the first
                 tee in ten minutes! I'm playing with the
                 council's Chief Executive Officer ... we
                 need him on board vis-à-vis the drainage
                 problem.

LAURA            What about your mother?

SIMON            I know, I know. But when I took on the role
                 of Secretary I always knew that personal
                 sacrifices would have to be made. I can't
                 let the side down. Still, I know I can rely
                 on you, Laura ... a good team ... that's
                 what we are ... a bloomin' good team. Give

her my love ... buy her some flowers or
something.

(LAURA *is open mouthed and speechless.*
SIMON *gives her a peck on the cheek
and then strides off towards the bar. He
suddenly stops in mid-track.*)

(*turning back and pointing at* LAURA *with
a grimace*) Leaking urinal. I knew there
was something. (*With a sudden flash of
inspiration.*) How do you think your flood
chap's fixed? See if you can get him down
here. Second urinal on the left.

(*Satisfied with the solution,* SIMON *strides
off towards the bar again. He stops and
turns back to* LAURA *just before exiting.*)
You're a rock, Laura ...you know that?
(*Moving to* TIFFANY.) That woman is a saint.

(SIMON *exits, leaving* LAURA *and* TIFFANY
*looking after him. They finally look at each
other.*)

LAURA        Good. Saint is it?

TIFFANY      He seems to think so.

LAURA        Do I look like the patron saint of bloody
             plumbing?

TIFFANY      I don't know ... I didn't realise there was
             one.

LAURA        Well ... (*Looking around and seeing the
             spade leaning against the table she moves
             to it and picks it up, smiling demonically.*)
             ... we'll see about saint.

(LAURA *puts the spade over her shoulder
and marches determinedly off onto the
course.* TIFFANY *watches her with growing
unease.*)

TIFFANY          What are you going to do? (*Moving centre
stage and calling after* LAURA.) Excuse me
… excuse me … I don't think that's allowed
really … no, you mustn't, that's one of
their putting pitches … oh, dear, you're not
going to go too deep are you … I'll tell you
what, I'll just fetch someone shall I? … (*To
herself, pulling a face, out front.*) … Oops!

(TIFFANY *runs into the bar as … the lights
fade.*)

## ACT TWO

### Scene One

*Mid afternoon, the same day. The tables are littered with
empty drinks containers and used paper plates.* LAURA
*is sitting at one of the tables on the terrace reading a
woman's magazine, and has a glass of wine in front of
her on the table together with an empty wine bottle. She
is not drunk but has clearly drunk enough to remove any
inhibitions. During the course of the scene, the alcohol
gradually has more and more effect.* TIFFANY *has pulled two
chairs together to form a sun-lounger and has a slice of
cucumber covering each eye.*

| | |
|---|---|
| LAURA | (*muttering to herself*) Bloody ridiculous! |
| TIFFANY | What is? |
| | (LAURA *flings the magazine on to the table and takes a sip of wine before glancing at* TIFFANY.) |
| LAURA | Do you know what's wrong with this country? |
| TIFFANY | I think Nick could give you a list. He says it all started going wrong with emancipation … (*Reflecting.*) except he calls it emancip-i-ation … he's not very good with long words. |
| LAURA | Yes, I'd noticed. Simon could write a book about long words. In fact, if he ever *wrote* a book … heaven help us … it would consist *entirely* of long words. Nothing fewer than three syllables. |

TIFFANY        (*sitting up and removing the slices of
               cucumber*) He didn't seem very pleased
               about you digging up the putting pitch.

LAURA          (*smiling to herself*) No he didn't. (*With an
               expression of mock horror.*) I expect when
               he gets me home he'll knock me about ... be
               terribly brutal and forceful.

TIFFANY        (*shocked*) He won't will he?

LAURA          No, Tiffany, he won't. Sometimes I almost
               wish he would. It would be some kind of
               acknowledgement that I actually exist ...
               that he cared enough to bother. No, he'll
               probably send me a three page memo
               instructing that I don't do it again unless
               I consult the appropriate sub-committee.
               That's Simon's way ... the orderly civilised
               way.

TIFFANY        Nick wouldn't dare hit *me*. I'd kill him ...
               (*With feeling.*) I would *so* kill him.

LAURA          I wouldn't dare kill Simon. He'd come back
               and haunt me, Scrooge only had to put up
               with the ghost of Christmas Past ... I'd have
               the ghost of bloody tedium past.

TIFFANY        (*not sure how to react, standing, putting the
               cucumber slices on the chair and moving
               to* LAURA) Have you finished with my
               magazine?

LAURA          Oh, yes, thank you. That was very rude of
               me ... but that's what set me off.

TIFFANY        Sorry, I thought you might like it. (*Glancing
               down at the open magazine and imitating a
               series of unlikely model postures.*) It has all

the latest gossip on the celebs. I'd like to be famous but I can't do anything.

LAURA        But that's exactly the point, Tiffany. The trouble with this country is that the less you can do, the better off you are. If you want to be a celebrity just go on some reality TV show.

TIFFANY      (*finishing her model postures and sitting next to* LAURA) It'd be dead good to be in there though. I sometimes wish I wore glasses. It would make me look more intelligent. What do you think?

LAURA        Not necessary. The link between all those people is that they're all mindless, unashamed morons with the IQ of a vacuum cleaner.

TIFFANY      (*brightly*) There's hope for Nick then.

LAURA        (*probing*) You and Nick ...?

TIFFANY      Yeah?

             (LAURA *simply looks at her questioningly.*)

             You don't get it either do you. (*Laughing.*) All my friends think I'm mad ... (*Pulling a face.*) He's so old!

LAURA        How long have you ...?

TIFFANY      'Bout a year now. We met in a lay-by.

LAURA        What?

TIFFANY      My car broke down. Nick stopped on his bike to see if I needed any help. It was

dead funny really ... he pulled up in front
of me, hit a litter bin and fell off. Bit of a
character.

LAURA          Isn't he just.

               (TIFFANY *looks questioning.*)

               (*smiling slightly*) Oh, I used to know him
               quite well ... not so much these days.

TIFFANY        I know we're always having a go at each
               other but ... underneath it all I think he's
               the kindest man I've ever met. My best
               friend. (*Giggling.*) And I think he's great at
               ... you know what ... for an old bloke!

LAURA          (*raising her eyebrows*) Really? (*Reflecting.*)
               You surprise me.

               (NICK *and* BARRY *enter from the course.*)

NICK           All I'm saying is, you could have backed me
               up a bit.

BARRY          (*indignant*) Me back *you* up!

NICK           Alright Tiffs?

               (NICK *moves to* TIFFANY. BARRY *notices the
               two cucumber slices lying on the chair,
               pops them into his mouth and chews
               contentedly.*)

TIFFANY        I'd rather be out buying shoes.

NICK           You've already got more shoes than feet ...
               what's the point of that?

| | |
|---|---|
| TIFFANY | Because, Nick, you need different shoes for different outfits. |
| NICK | Well, get rid of some outfits then. |
| TIFFANY | And then what would I do with all my handbags, stupid? |
| NICK | It's a mystery, Bas. How does a woman's mind work? |
| BARRY | (*glancing pointedly at* LAURA) No point asking me, Nick. How would I know? |
| TIFFANY | Where have you two been anyway? You should have finished ages ago. |
| NICK | (*moving to the food table and getting himself a drink*) We stayed to a-judge-icate on the longest drive competition on the eighteenth. Just as well we did 'cos we had to break up a fight. |
| LAURA | Oh dear, fight on the hallowed fairways? Simon won't be happy! |
| NICK | Don't know about that ... *he* started it. |
| LAURA | *My* Simon? |
| BARRY | Big Frank Porterhouse started having a go about you digging up the green. Simon threatened to have him thrown out so he called Simon a pompous, anally retentive oaf. |
| LAURA | (*nodding*) Good description ... perceptive man. I've never known Simon fight though. |

BARRY        Oh, I think that was more of a
             misunderstanding. (*Miming a gun fighter.*)
             Simon went for his notebook and Frank hit
             him. Simon went at him like a rabid dog.

NICK         More like a sedated pussy cat.

BARRY        Even so ... fair play ... Frank's a big lad.

NICK         (*dismissive*) Barry, he's the least fit member
             in the club. What you've got there is a
             twenty stone beer belly on a six stone
             frame! Still, credit where it's due ... once
             he's on the move it'd be like trying to stop
             an articulate lorry. Anyway, we managed to
             split them up.

BARRY        Actually, *I* split them up while Nick tried to
             hide behind the flag pole.

NICK         (*indignant*) No I didn't ... I was just keeping
             it safe.

LAURA        (*mildly concerned*) Is Simon alright?

BARRY        Oh, he's fine. He might have broken his
             pencil but that's about it.

LAURA        I never realised golf could be so exciting.
             How did *your* game go, Barry? (*Pointedly.*)
             Or is that an *unfair* question?

BARRY        (*trying not to rise to the bait*) It is actually.
             Same as usual ... a series of tragedies
             punctuated with the odd miracle.

NICK         And don't forget the ninety quid you owe
             me for the driver.

BARRY          You must be joking ... I'm not giving you anything!

NICK           A deal's a deal, Barry. We shook hands on it.

BARRY          (*carrying one of* TIFFANY'S *chairs closer to* LAURA *and* TIFFANY, *and sitting on it*) No we didn't. Anyway, I don't care ... I'm not paying you.

NICK           Well, to be honest, I'm disappointed in you Bas. Still, if you want to renegade on it, just give me it back in its original condition and we'll say no more.

BARRY          But you know I can't. (*To* TIFFANY *and* LAURA.) It broke in half the second time I used it.

NICK           That's because you hit something with it.

BARRY          I hit the *ball* with it!

NICK           Which just shows what a good club it was ... you normally miss by a foot! (*To* TIFFANY.) Thought you might have got this lot cleared up by now.

TIFFANY        Me?

NICK           If you want to enjoy yourself tonight you don't want this lot hanging around.

TIFFANY        Well, you can help me then.

NICK           And I'd like to Tiffs, but to be honest I haven't got the time. Bas and I need to get all the score cards checked and sorted in numberlogical order before the evening's festivities.

(SIMON *enters. He is looking cheerful and buoyant and has a broad grin on his face.*)

SIMON
Ah, here you are, Nicholas. Marvellous day, eh? (*Moving to* NICK *and shaking his hand.*) Just wanted to thank you. Didn't think you had it in you but ... well done ... enough said?

(*During the following passage* SIMON *moves around the patio and between various characters. Every time he passes* BARRY *he has to walk around him and he becomes increasingly irritated by* BARRY'S *untidy chair positioning. After several 'passes' he pointedly stops in front of* BARRY *and gestures for him to move his chair in towards the table.*)

NICK
No problem. Hate to see grown men with handbags drawn.

SIMON
What ... Fatty Porterhouse? Oh, I think I showed him what's what. He'll not be trying that sort of nonsense again. (*Patting his pocket with satisfaction.*) I've got his name in the book.

LAURA
I hear you were standing up for me, darling. (*Genuine.*) Thank you.

SIMON
Oh, nothing really. (*Turning his attention back to* NICK.) No, what I actually meant was the organisation of the day ... don't want to labour the point but ... first class. Well done.

NICK
(*stunned*) Me? (*Modestly.*) To be honest I haven't done anything really.

| | |
|---|---|
| SIMON | And all the better for it. A light touch is always the best policy in my view. There's still time for the whole thing to go pear-shaped of course but, so far so good. |
| LAURA | You seem to be in a remarkably good mood, Simon. |
| SIMON | And why wouldn't I be? Beautiful day ... good company ... (*As an after thought.*) ... charming wife ... (*Casually.*) and only the best bloomin' round of my life. (*Proudly.*) Net sixty five. That should take the individual prize I think? |
| BARRY | (*glum*) Well done. I had a net ninety two. |
| LAURA | I'm sure it's the taking part that counts, Barry. Don't take any notice of my husband ... he's a terrible gloater. |
| SIMON | (*between gritted teeth*) Not true, my love. Not true at all. |
| LAURA | Yes you are ... you gloat at the drop of a hat. |
| SIMON | Hardly. There's a difference between gloating and quiet satisfaction in a job well done. Point taken? Net sixty five though, that'll take some beating eh? Sixty five. |
| | (SIMON *looks around expectantly for congratulations, but the others ignore him.*) |
| | Net sixty five, Nicholas. Probably just pipped you eh? |
| NICK | (*offhand, sulky, clearly annoyed to have been beaten*) It's not bad I suppose. To be |

|          | honest I wasn't that bothered … it's all about the day really. |
|----------|-----------------------------------------------------------------|
| SIMON    | Oh, exactly my point. (*Leaning super-casually against the back of the chair* TIFFANY *is sitting on.*) Still … net sixty five … what do you think to that, Tiffany? |
| TIFFANY  | (*pulling a face*) I don't know what it means, Simon. What do you use a net for? |
| NICK     | It means he's a bandit … that's what it means! |
| SIMON    | Not true … hard earned, dogged performance I'd say. (*Shaking his head in wonder.*) Bloomin' sixty five! |
| LAURA    | (*losing patience*) Will you stop going on about it? It's only a number! |
| SIMON    | (*defensive*) Quite a low one though. (*Proudly.*) Did I mention that I was nearest the pin as well? |
| LAURA    | What on earth are you talking about? |
| SIMON    | (*miming the shot and visualising the ball soaring into the distance*) Seventh hole … par three. Nearest the hole with their tee shot wins a prize. |
| NICK     | (*smiling to himself*) Ah, but it wasn't you though. |
| SIMON    | Afraid it was. We were the last ones through and I was clearly the winner by six hundred and twenty three millimetres. |

| | |
|---|---|
| NICK | Yes, but after that, Barry here got closer … cracking shot too. To be honest, I didn't think he had it in him. |
| SIMON | Oh no, impossible. You played that hole a long time before me. |
| NICK | Yes, but Barry's attempt at the longest drive on the eighteenth went sideways across two fairways and landed right next to the flag on the seventh. |
| BARRY | (*apologetically*) Bit of a shank. I don't think it counts really, Nick. |
| NICK | Rubbish, I'm in charge and I'm allowing it. |
| SIMON | But you can't! He wasn't on the correct hole. |
| NICK | He was rarely (*Mimicking* SIMON.) "on the correct hole" all the way round but I don't give a bugger. |
| SIMON | No, I can't have that … that's a flagrant breech of the rules of the competition. |
| LAURA | Don't be churlish, darling, you can't expect to win everything. (*Pointedly.*) It wouldn't be *fair* would it, Barry? |
| BARRY | Let's just leave it shall we? |
| SIMON | (*to* NICK) I shall be putting in an objection. |
| LAURA | And my husband can be *very* objectionable, as you well know, Nick. |
| SIMON | (*frowning at* LAURA) Actually, I'm surprised you're still here, my love. (*Looking* |

*suspiciously at the bottle*.) Still, I suppose you couldn't rush your bottle of wine ... I see you opted for the most expensive.

LAURA        I put it on your bar bill.

SIMON        (*with a grimace*) Excellent. (*Doubtfully*.) Still, nothing but the best eh? Suppose you'll have to leave your car here. Shall I call you a taxi?

LAURA        No, I've decided to stay for the dinner.

SIMON        What? But you can't. I mean, what about the numbers ... we'll be out.

LAURA        The chef said it's not a problem.

SIMON        Did he?

LAURA        Yes, darling, so no need to worry. And incidentally, there's been no further news of your mother, so you can rest easy I think.

SIMON        Ah ... good ... excellent. Well done.

LAURA        You've clearly been fretting about her.

SIMON        Ah ... yes. Didn't want to put a dampener on everyone else's day though. Stiff upper lip.

TIFFANY      We'll all be able to sit at the same table and have a bit of a laugh won't we, Nick?

NICK         (*who can think of nothing worse*) Oh, brilliant. Can't wait. To be honest, Simon's like one of the Chuckle Brothers when he gets going.

FRAN            (*shouting, from the bar*) Ah, Weaver, there
                you are.

                (SIMON *watches nervously as* FRAN *enters
                from the bar.*)

                Finally tracked you down. Hear you had a
                good round.

SIMON           (*modestly*) Oh nothing really ... few good
                bounces ... (*Slightly furtive.*) ... lucky
                to find the odd lost ball. Best round ever
                actually but no point going on about it ...
                net sixty five.

FRAN            (*fiercely*) And do you know what the best
                ladies score was on the thirteenth with that
                blessed ornamental bush?

SIMON           (*guessing hopefully*) Three?

FRAN            Eight ... it's impossible ... it takes three
                shots to work round it.

BARRY           I took twelve.

FRAN            It's totally unacceptable. I've taken a quick
                straw poll of the ladies and we demand
                immediate action. Either the bush goes or
                we do.

SIMON           What do you mean?

FRAN            We shall all leave the club and move
                somewhere more accommodating.

SIMON           But you can't! I mean, what about your
                membership fees? We rely on them.

FRAN            Exactly, Weaver ... you need us more than
                we need you. Do I make myself clear? We
                require a decision today.

SIMON           (*flustered*) But that's impossible. Do you
                realise how many committee stages would
                be involved in making that kind of decision?
                The amount of paperwork required would
                be staggering.

BARRY           They have got a point, Simon.

NICK            And Bas should know ... he is an honorary
                lady for the day.

FRAN            No time like the present. There are a few
                committee types in the bar. I suggest you go
                and have a word.

SIMON           Oh, no, no ... I'm afraid it's out of the
                question.

FRAN            Did I mention that we also plan a
                demonstration in the middle of the dinner?

SIMON           (*alarmed*) A what?

FRAN            Mrs Cob has threatened to start it off with a
                streak during the entrée.

SIMON           (*horrified*) Mrs Cob? But she's grotesque!

BARRY           And the wrong side of seventy.

NICK            To be fair, she came into her own at the
                Halloween supper though.

FRAN            You'd best go with him, Armitage ... I'm
                sure I can rely on your support.

| | |
|---|---|
| NICK | Fair enough. Come on Simon ... it's your chance to have an extra meeting and you know how much you like them. I can only spare ten minutes mind, so you can't waffle on like normal. You'll have to make a start on the score cards by yourself, Bas. |

(BARRY *stands*.)

| | |
|---|---|
| SIMON | (*pushing down on* BARRY'S *shoulder, forcing him to sit*) But he's not authorised! |
| NICK | (*pulling* BARRY *back up into a standing position*) Well, you can lend him your official rubber stamp ... we won't tell anyone. |
| LAURA | And you can buy me another little drink on the way. |

(LAURA *rises from her chair and takes* SIMON'S *arm to lead him inside*.)

Apparently you've reached your credit limit at the bar.

| | |
|---|---|
| SIMON | (*as he reluctantly exits to the bar*) This is all highly irregular. It's tantamount to anarchy. |

(SIMON *and* LAURA *exit to the bar, closely followed by* NICK *and* BARRY.)

| | |
|---|---|
| BARRY | (*as he exits*) What am I supposed to do with the score cards? |
| NICK | Just pray you find one lower than Simon's or we'll never hear the end of it. |

(TIFFANY *and* FRAN *are left alone*.)

FRAN

(*satisfied*) That's the way to handle Weaver's type. No point pussyfooting.

TIFFANY

Were all the ladies *really* going to stage a demo?

FRAN

Couldn't tell you ... haven't spoken to any of them.

TIFFANY

You mean it was all a fib? That's brilliant.

FRAN

I prefer to think of it as a tactical flanking manoeuvre.

TIFFANY

Still brilliant though. (*Sighing and moving to the food table.*) I suppose I'd better sort this lot out. Nick *so* does my head in.

FRAN

Want a hand?

TIFFANY

Wouldn't mind.

(*They both move to the table and start to tidy things away. Through the following dialogue they gradually move things into various boxes and piles and rearrange the patio furniture.* TIFFANY *is still clearly intrigued by* FRAN'S *sexuality and keeps glancing at her in curiosity as she chatters nervously.* FRAN *can't help but notice* TIFFANY'S *glances and is totally bemused by them. They exchange occasional uneasy smiles.*)

I'm going to be an air hostess ... Nick says I'll just be doing this sort of stuff all day, you know, serving people, but there's much more to it than that.

FRAN

Yes, I expect there is.

(FRAN *starts placing several items, including an empty wine bottle, into a cardboard box.*)

TIFFANY    Yeah. You have to know where the emergency exits are and everything really. I suppose they probably like you to know how to fly as well ... in case you accidentally poison the pilots. I think I'd be quite good at that.

FRAN    Flying or poisoning?

TIFFANY    (*pulling a face*) Both probably. I expect I'd find flying quite easy ... I mean I took to riding a bicycle really really quickly.

FRAN    That's encouraging then.

TIFFANY    Cabin crew, that's the official title ... I quite like that ... cabin *crew* ... it can be men as well as women these days ... some people think that all the men who do it must be, you know, a bit like that ... (*Wide-eyed, realizing what she has said.*) ... but I'm sure they're not ... (*Thinking she has gone deeper, she starts talking more rapidly and in an increasingly high pitched voice. Unthinkingly, in a panic, she also starts rapidly unpacking the box that* FRAN *has been filling.*) ... and even if they were it wouldn't matter to me ... I mean, it takes all sorts doesn't it ... and people are just people really ... it doesn't matter about all their bits ... (*Stopping dead, empty wine bottle in hand, realising what she has just said.*) ... Oops ... I'm sorry, I don't think I meant that ... sorry.

FRAN            (*studying* TIFFANY *closely and taking the
                wine bottle from her*) Do you have some
                kind of problem with me, Tiffany?

TIFFANY         Me? Silly idea. Why would you think that?


FRAN            (*repacking the box*) That's fine then. You
                just seem a bit … excited.

TIFFANY         No, not at all.

                (*There is a slight pause as* FRAN
                *works busily.* TIFFANY *more slowly and
                thoughtfully.*)

                (*conversationally*) Have you been a member
                here long?

FRAN            I got posted back to the area a couple of
                years ago. I knew the club because I played
                here as a kid.

TIFFANY         Oh. Things have changed a bit since then I
                suppose … you know … *you've* changed.

FRAN            You could say that, yes. (*Smiling.*) I was just
                one of the lads in those days … all mucked
                in together.

TIFFANY         Lovely.

                (*There are a few moments of silence as they
                both continue to work.*)

                It's just that … (*Her curiosity finally
                getting the better of her.*) I hope you don't
                mind me asking, but I'm really interested in
                what you've done.

FRAN            Fire away. I don't mind.

TIFFANY         (*nervously*) I mean, I can see why people
                like you might like dressing up ... is it
                alright to say that? I suppose it's not *that*
                uncommon, but you've kind of gone all the
                way.

FRAN            Well, I don't wear a uniform *all* the time ...
                it's not necessary.

TIFFANY         No, I meant more like ... (*Embarrassed,
                almost whispering.*) ... operations.

FRAN            Ops?

TIFFANY         Yes. I just wondered ... have you ...
                (*Wiggling her hips.*) you know?

FRAN            Well ... yes. I have *been* in theatre
                obviously but there's nothing particularly
                remarkable about that.

TIFFANY         But weren't you worried about it all going
                wrong or something?

FRAN            No, not really. I suppose everybody gets a
                bit nervous before their first one, but I felt
                like I was ready for it.

TIFFANY         And I suppose it's not that dangerous really.

FRAN            Well, there are no guarantees but ...
                statistically no.

TIFFANY         And you don't have any regrets?

FRAN            No, of course not. It's something I wanted
                to do since I was quite young. (*Laughing.*)

My mother was in the Forces and I was
always dressing up in her old uniforms.

TIFFANY        And it all just went from there?

FRAN           Yes, I suppose so. When I was in my late
               teens I just did it part-time, on a weekend.
               It was great. You met all sorts from factory
               workers to solicitors.

TIFFANY        (*wide eyed*) All dressing up?

FRAN           (*laughing*) Yes, but there's a bit more to it
               than that. There's plenty of action if you're
               up for it.

TIFFANY        (*open mouthed*) Really? It's like another
               world.

FRAN           I got so hooked on it that I eventually
               decided to go the whole hog.

TIFFANY        I bet your dad wasn't very pleased?

FRAN           Oh, he was great. When I made the final
               decision to really go for it, he wasn't that
               keen, but he said that if it was what I
               wanted to do, it was fine with him.

TIFFANY        Really? I think that's ever so sweet. Very
               supportive.

FRAN           (*fondly*) Yes, he's always been there for
               me. I mean, I think deep down he always
               wanted me to be a boy but he gradually
               came round. These days he always says he
               doesn't know where he'd be without his
               little girl.

TIFFANY        Nice.

FRAN            Don't suppose you've ever considered a
                change?

TIFFANY         No, not at all. I'm quite happy as I am.

FRAN            It's just with you mentioning an interest in
                flying. You could join the brylcreem boys.

TIFFANY         Not really me.

                (BARRY *enters from the bar.*)

BARRY           Hard at work?

TIFFANY         Hi Barry. We were just having a nice chat.

BARRY           Really? I don't seem to be able to have
                those.

                (BARRY *looks at* FRAN, *removes his
                spectacles and tries to casually slip them
                into a top pocket.*)

                (*in what he considers to be a suave and
                manly voice*) Can I get you a drink or
                anything?

                (BARRY *realises that he doesn't have a top
                pocket and smiles, embarrassed.*)

FRAN            I thought you were supposed to be doing
                things with score cards?

BARRY           No, Nick said he could manage on his own.

FRAN            But he's in a committee meeting.

BARRY           All dead in the water I'm afraid. Never got
                off the ground.

| | |
|---|---|
| FRAN | (*exploding*) What? |
| BARRY | Simon had a count up and decided they weren't quorate ... you know what he's like. |
| FRAN | Right, I've had just about enough of this club. (*Thinking hard.*) West, Tiffany ... with me. We'll show them we mean business. |
| BARRY | But it's not really anything to do with me. |
| FRAN | Nonsense. (*To* TIFFANY.) Can you handle a chain saw? |
| TIFFANY | Not really. I'm a bit off them after my Gran's accident. |
| FRAN | You can drive the tractor then. Come on ... we need to move quickly and decisively if we're going to pull it off. Follow me. |

(FRAN *hurries off towards the Green Keeper's compound, followed uncertainly by* BARRY *and* TIFFANY.)

| | |
|---|---|
| TIFFANY | (*as she exits*) Where are we going? |
| BARRY | (*as he exits*) I'm not sure this is such a good idea. |

(*A few seconds later,* LAURA *enters from the bar carrying a drink. She is now noticeably rather drunk.* SIMON *hovers just inside the doorway.*)

| | |
|---|---|
| LAURA | (*impatient*) Come on, Simon, it's quite safe, she's gone. |

(SIMON *follows* LAURA *out, nervously.*)

I don't know why you're frightened of her.

SIMON    (*indignant*) What a ridiculous thought. It's just that there's little merit in allowing her to cause a scene ... today of all days. Her grievances will just have to wait. Fair comment? Point taken?

LAURA    (*sitting at a table and sipping at her drink*) It's not *me* you need to convince.

SIMON    I don't see why you wanted to come out here again anyway.

LAURA    I wanted to come out because it's *stuffy* in there.

SIMON    (*puzzled*) Shouldn't be ... we've just had the air-con serviced. If they've bloomin' well messed it up again I'll ...

LAURA    It's stuffy because of the *people*, not the air! I've never seen such a load of miserable, grumpy old gits.

SIMON    Some of them are very good friends of mine.

LAURA    Exactly ... hardly a shining accolade. And if you say (*Imitating* SIMON.) "Oh, just a sixty five" one more time ... it hardly makes you Rory Macintosh or whatever his name is.

SIMON    Well you don't have to be here, Laura. You insisted on staying. Personally I'd have thought you'd have preferred to call in on mother and then get home to sort out the flood damage but ... (*Shrugging helplessly.*) ... anyway, I won't labour the point ... you

know best. It's not as if the ambience of the
clubhouse should come as any surprise to
you ... I've tried to get you to integrate but,
no. Still, not your fault I suppose.

LAURA        *I* don't integrate?

SIMON        Not noticeably ... not as the Club
             Secretary's wife might be expected, but
             I'll not press the point. I expect that many
             wives would relish the opportunity to hold
             such a privileged position but, if you don't
             care to support me, that's your prerogative.

LAURA        (*standing and talking loudly*) How have you
             got the nerve? How have you got the *bloody*
             nerve?

SIMON        Careful, Laura, people will hear.

LAURA        So let them listen. What do I care? Let *them*
             integrate.

SIMON        (*pointing at her glass*) I knew it was a
             mistake you having a double ... best make
             that your last.

LAURA        It's a treble ... I asked the sweet boy behind
             the bar for a treble. He's quite fanciable
             actually.

SIMON        (*shocked*) He's half your age! He's the
             vicar's son!

LAURA        So?

SIMON        (*looking around, embarrassed*) Look, I
             think I'd best order you a taxi before you
             get too giddy. No point making a scene
             here.

(*Through the following passage,* SIMON *is distracted as he starts to fiddle with his mobile, finding a taxi number, pressing a key to connect and listening for a reply, all the time trying to make sure that nobody else can hear what is happening.*)

LAURA            So you're saying that *I* don't integrate?

SIMON            (*smiling, pacifying*) Not really, my love, but clearly that's not important.

LAURA            And I suppose *you* do?

SIMON            I try my best ... try to maintain a broad circle.

LAURA            So what about *my* friends and *my* family? What about them?

SIMON            Not exactly my types but ...

LAURA            You don't even *know* my friends, Simon, because you're not remotely interested.

SIMON            Not true.

LAURA            (*loud*) You treat my friends like lepers and you treat my family like shit!

SIMON            (SIMON'S *eyes widen in alarm*) Laura! (SIMON *looks around quickly, spots someone off, waves and calls over to them, apologetically.*) Hello, Derek ... sorry about that ... (*Shrugging, smiling apologetically and pointing at* LAURA.) ... the wife. (*Urgently, to* LAURA.) ... that's the bloomin' Mayor! (*Calling off again.*) I'll let you have one of our new club ties ... no charge ... on me.

LAURA            (*calling and waving off*) Hello, Derek. He
                 messed up on the ties actually, but he said
                 they'd look alright on little short-arses like
                 you.

                 (SIMON *stands in open-mouthed shock.*)

                 (*to* SIMON) Was that being friendly enough,
                 darling? (*Calling off again.*) Incidentally,
                 Derek, I voted for your lot ... but he didn't
                 ... he says you're all weasely corrupt
                 little toe rags. (*Mimicking the way* SIMON
                 *shrugged, smiled and pointed.*) ... the
                 husband. (*Waving, blowing a kiss and
                 speaking suggestively.*) See you later, you
                 little sex pot you.

SIMON            (*still shocked but realizing that someone is
                 speaking on the phone, answering*) ... Ah,
                 sorry ... hello ... Sorry about that ... is that
                 Budget Taxis? ...

                 (LAURA *moves to* SIMON, *grabs the phone
                 from him and speaks into it, moving out of
                 reach of* SIMON.)

LAURA            ... Hello ... My husband wished to enquire
                 whether you had a taxi currently available
                 ... You have? ... Well, that's your own fault
                 for having too many on duty at the same
                 time. Fair comment? Enough said? Point
                 taken? Excellent. Thank you so much.
                 (LAURA *triumphantly presses a key to ring
                 off and hands the phone back to* SIMON.)
                 Isn't this fun ... integrating?

                 (SIMON *gazes at* LAURA *in shock, speechless
                 and horrified.*)

I haven't enjoyed myself so much for simply ages. I must be having one of my *tetchy* moments.

SIMON     I really don't know what's got in to you. You were like this last Christmas.

LAURA     Was I, darling? I really can't remember. Oh yes, there was that strange man in the house.

SIMON     (*mystified*) No there wasn't.

LAURA     Wasn't there? Oh, silly old me ... that was *you* wasn't it. The golf club isn't open on Christmas Day and we spent the whole day together and I got drunk and embarrassed you in front of that mad woman ... sorry, your dear mother.

SIMON     Look, we've been through that before. Enough said. No point going over old ground. All I ask is that you behave yourself while you're here ... don't want to be shown up ... not too much to ask.

LAURA     Would you like to know how much I *really* integrate, Simon?

SIMON     This is ridiculous. I wish I hadn't mentioned it ...

LAURA     You'd be surprised how well I get on with *some* of the members. I know some of them *very* well. Don't you ever wonder for a teeny-weeny moment what I do when you're here every bloody hour that God sends?

(SIMON *stiffens but remains silent.*)

You'd be surprised how some of them
enjoy a few hours relaxation away from the
course. Even *on* the course for that matter.

SIMON         That's enough, Laura. You've had your little
joke now, so we'll say no more about it.
Point made. Message received ...

LAURA         ... and understood? I don't think so.
Wouldn't you like names, Simon? Wouldn't
you like details? You always like details.
You could write them down in that bloody
stupid little note book of yours. So stuff
you, Simon ... stuff you!

(SIMON *remains silent, traumatised and
totally lost as to how to resolve the
situation.* LAURA *suddenly lurches to one
side and giggles.*)

SIMON         Laura?

LAURA         I don't think I feel very well. It must be the
sun. I think I'll have a little sit down for a
minute.

(LAURA *gropes her way towards one of the
chairs.* SIMON *watches for a moment and
then moves to her and tries to help her in to
a chair.*)

What are you doing?

SIMON         Just helping, my love.

LAURA         I don't need your bloody help.

(LAURA *collapses into the chair, holding her
head, as* BARRY *rushes in from the car park.
He is in a complete panic.*)

| | |
|---|---|
| BARRY | Nick ... where's Nick? |
| SIMON | Still inside I think. |
| BARRY | (*rushing past*) I need to find him ... there's been a terrible accident. |

(BARRY *races past, into the bar, as* SIMON *looks on, worried.*)

| | |
|---|---|
| LAURA | (*looking up*) Was that Barry? Did I hear Barry? |
| SIMON | Yes, my love. |
| LAURA | Well I've integrated with *him* so you can put him in your little book. Number three I think. |

(LAURA *hiccups and slumps down with her head in her hands as the lights fade.*)


### Scene Two

*Early evening, the same day. The table has been removed from the putting green.* BARRY *is sitting outside drinking a beer from a pint glass. His shirt is untucked.* FRAN *enters from the course. She wears a hi-viz vest and carries a pair of gloves and a chainsaw safety helmet. She has a dirty face and hands. She sees* BARRY *and moves to join him. Their relationship has subtly changed and they are becoming more aware of each other.*

| | |
|---|---|
| FRAN | Alright, West? |
| BARRY | Yes, fine I suppose. |
| FRAN | I've finished logging up. |

BARRY        Oh, good.

FRAN         Probably enough there to see someone through the winter.

BARRY       (*nodding*) Big bush.

                (FRAN *takes* BARRY'S *beer and finishes it in one gulp.* BARRY *watches in surprise.*)

FRAN         (*sitting next to* BARRY) Thirsty work. I'll get you another one in a minute.

BARRY       Fine.

                (*They sit in silence for a few seconds.*)

FRAN         Good job done.

BARRY       Yeah. Tiffs accident takes the shine off it though. I feel a bit responsible really.

FRAN         Nonsense ... not your fault at all. If anybody bears the blame, it's me ... it *was* all my idea.

BARRY       I mean, I only turned my back for a moment. I heard her scream and when I looked round she was just lying there ... crushed, mangled. It was like everything was happening in slow motion.

FRAN         (*putting a comforting hand on his arm*) Not to worry ... chin up.

                (NICK *appears at the doorway to the bar. He has changed for the evening dinner and wears what he considers to be a 'trendy' jacket and one of the new club ties which is untidily knotted with the thin end hanging*

(*down longer than the thick end.* NICK *is
furious and distraught and frowns fiercely
when he sees* BARRY *and* FRAN *sitting
outside.*)

NICK        Ah … Skulking out here are you. You ought
            to be ashamed of yourselves, the pair of
            you. I mean, to be honest, I know Barry's
            a bloody liability but I'm surprised at you
            Fran.

FRAN        Any news?

NICK        I've just been on to them now. They reckon
            she's got no chance … terminal.

BARRY       Surely not!

NICK        (*turning his head into the bar and shouting*)
            Hey … Farmer Giles … out here.

            (NICK *steps outside and his place in the
            doorway is taken by* TIFFANY.)

TIFFANY     What?

NICK        Tell 'em about the bike.

BARRY       It can't be a write off, surely?

TIFFANY     (*pulling a face*) Yeah, I'm afraid it's like …
            oops!

NICK        What were you thinking of, letting her drive
            a tractor? She can hardly drive a shopping
            trolley!

FRAN        That's my fault. I thought everyone knew
            how to drive one.

BARRY            I don't.

TIFFANY          (*indignant*) I was doing really well, Nick …
                 reversing and everything. I only swerved
                 'cos Barry threw himself in front of me

BARRY            I did not! I was just going to collect a stray
                 golf ball I spotted in the hedge bottom.

TIFFANY          It's dead lucky your bike bore the brunt
                 really, Nick, 'cos it sort of slowed me down
                 a bit before I hit Simon's BMW. (*Brightly.*)
                 His crumple zone worked really well.

NICK             Never mind his car … what about my bike?

BARRY            Sorry, mate. (*Reaching in his pocket and
                 producing a golf ball*). You can have the
                 ball if you like … it's a really nice Nike.

                 (NICK *scowls at* BARRY *but takes the ball
                 from him.*)

TIFFANY          The bike never really suited you, Nick …
                 you should get a little moped or something.

NICK             (*moving to sit at the other table*) I don't
                 *want* a moped. Anyway, unless somebody
                 coughs up for it I won't even be able to
                 afford a skate board.

FRAN             You'll have to claim on the insurance.

NICK             Well, I can't claim on *mine* 'cos I haven't
                 got any.

TIFFANY          Nick! I've been on the back of that bike!

| | |
|---|---|
| NICK | Well, you didn't fall off! To be honest, there didn't seem to be much point insuring it until I got it taxed and MOT'd. |
| TIFFANY | Nick! |
| NICK | It's no good 'Nick-ing' me ... that's not going to help. |
| BARRY | I hope Simon's insured. |
| TIFFANY | (*pulling a face*) I don't think we should tell him about his car 'til later. |
| | (*Unseen by them all,* SIMON *appears in the bar doorway just in time to hear* FRAN's *following remark. He has changed into shirt and tie but has no jacket.*) |
| FRAN | Knowing Weaver, he's certainly not going to be very pleased. |
| SIMON | Not going to be pleased about what? |
| | (BARRY, FRAN *and* TIFFANY *look round, guiltily and their three responses almost overlap.*) |
| TIFFANY | Oops! |
| BARRY | Nothing. |
| FRAN | The bush. |
| SIMON | Ah yes, the bush. (*Scowling.*) You still here, Barry? |
| BARRY | Yes. Why wouldn't I be? |

SIMON            (*brooding*) From what I hear you have
                 ... (*Choosing his words carefully.*) other
                 interests ... other activities. Still, I'm not
                 sure that any of you will be here much
                 longer.

NICK             Why not?

SIMON            Tampering with golf club flora and
                 equipment. Tantamount to vandalism in my
                 opinion but I won't labour the point. It's a
                 pity the four of you took it upon yourselves
                 to bypass the democratic process.

NICK             Don't bring *me* in to it, they flattened my
                 bike!

SIMON            Yes, I heard it had to be taken away. (*Trying
                 to suppress a smile and making footstep
                 gestures with his finguers.*) Perhaps you
                 may have to resort to more conventional
                 transport arrangements in future.

FRAN             I take full responsibility for everything,
                 Weaver ... no one else to blame.

SIMON            (*relishing his position of power*) Not quite
                 as simple as that I'm afraid. As I understand
                 it, you, Francis ... (*Glaring at* BARRY *and
                 pointedly emphasising his name.*) *Barry* and
                 young Tiffany were all involved. As Tiffany
                 was your guest, Nicholas, the club rules
                 clearly stipulate that you are held personally
                 responsible and accountable for all her
                 actions whilst on the premises.

NICK             What does that mean in English?

SIMON            It means that, in effect, you helped to fell
                 the bush and ran over your own motorcycle.

NICK            That's not fair!

SIMON           Out of my hands. I mean, she's only been
                here a day and she's practically wrecked the
                place.

FRAN            All nonsense. So what happens next?

SIMON           (*importantly*) Well, as Secretary I shall
                undertake a thorough investigation ...
                gather and weigh the full facts fairly and
                impartially ... and then submit a report
                recommending that *Barry* be expelled from
                the club.

BARRY           Why me? Surely you can swing it for us,
                Simon? You said earlier that we were your
                chums.

SIMON           Chums, Barry? A bit rich coming from you.

BARRY           Why, what have *I* done?

SIMON           Done? (*Stiffening.*) Let's just say that
                certain extra-curricula activities have been
                brought to my attention by my wife.

                (BARRY'S *jaw drops open.*)

                Point taken? Message received and
                understood? I'm disappointed, Barry ... but
                I'll not labour the point in mixed company.
                (*Turning to* FRAN *and* NICK.) As for you two,
                I must be seen to be impartial but I'll make
                a note to ensure that your previous good
                behaviour is considered in mitigation.

NICK            Can we claim on the club's insurance for my
                bike?

SIMON    (*pulling his notebook from his pocket*) Oh
         no ... out of the question. Unauthorised use
         of golf club equipment. (*Pointedly.*) Some
         of you may be *chums* but I can't sanction
         fraudulent claims. (*Writing in his notebook.*)
         ... Mit-i-gation ... Frances and Nicholas
         ... *not Barry.* (*Looking up, satisfied then
         noticing* NICK'S *tie.*) What's happened to
         your tie?

NICK     It's one of the new ones, they seem a bit of a
         funny shape.

SIMON    You shouldn't be wearing that, they've not
         been released yet.

NICK     Well, I forgot mine so Smithy lent me this.
         They're hardly going to be next season's
         fashion must-have.

SIMON    (*looking at the tie closely*) He's gone and
         got the wrong bloomin' motif as well!
         (*Sighing heavily.*) I don't know why I
         bother. (*Consulting his note book.*)

TIFFANY  How's Laura, I haven't seen her for a couple
         of hours?

SIMON    Laura? Erm ... just having a lie down in my
         office.

TIFFANY  (*sympathetic*) She had had a bit to drink.

SIMON    Oh, nothing like that, no ... just a touch of
         ... (*Searching for an acceptable ailment.*) ...
         migraine. (*Glancing at his notebook.*) Next
         on my list actually ... aspirin from car.

(SIMON *moves to exit to the car park.*
TIFFANY, BARRY *and* FRAN *exchange anxious*
*glances.*)

TIFFANY            (*eyes widening in panicking*) Your car? No
                   ... no, you musn't!

SIMON              Why ever not?

TIFFANY            Why? Well, because ... because you
                   shouldn't take aspirin with a migraine.

SIMON              First I've heard of that.

TIFFANY            (*struggling for an explanation*) No ... not
                   when it's been stored in a car ... in hot
                   weather ... it makes it go funny. I've got
                   something in my bag she can have.

SIMON              (*uncertain*) Ah, excellent. Well done. Just
                   get my jacket from the car then.

                   (SIMON *exits to the car park, leaving*
                   TIFFANY, BARRY *and* FRAN *watching after*
                   *him anxiously.*)

TIFFANY            Oops!

FRAN               (*philosophically*) I suppose he's got to find
                   out *sometime*.

TIFFANY            (*decisive*) Come on, Nick.

NICK               Where to?

TIFFANY            (*taking a packet of tablets from her*
                   *handbag*) You can show me where his office
                   is.

NICK               You can't hide for ever.

TIFFANY            No, but I can hide for a bit.

                   (NICK *shrugs and leads* TIFFANY *as they exit
                   back into the bar.*)

FRAN               (*glancing at* BARRY) Suppose we'd better
                   stay and face the music.

BARRY              I don't seem to be in his good books at all.

FRAN               Extra curricula activities eh? Do I detect a
                   hint of scandal?

BARRY              Something and nothing really. Extra
                   curricula for me but I suspect it's firmly on
                   Laura's regular timetable. (*Smiling sadly
                   to himself.*) But that's Laura ... always
                   searching for something extra but never
                   sure what she's actually looking for. Pity
                   she buggers up everybody else's life in the
                   process.

FRAN               Didn't realise you knew her so well.

BARRY              (*pulling a face*) I don't think I know her at
                   all. (*Reflective.*) Not sure that I want to.

                   (*During the following passage,* FRAN *and*
                   BARRY *are, by turns, reflective, sad, excited
                   and hopeful as they struggle to deal with
                   their feelings.*)

FRAN               (*looking at* BARRY *appraisingly*) You're a bit
                   of a dark horse, West. Never had you down
                   as a ladies' man.

BARRY              Me? You must be joking! Never had the
                   confidence.

FRAN               Snap.

| | |
|---|---|
| BARRY | Now I don't believe *that* for a minute. |
| FRAN | No ... true. Oh, when it comes to other things I'm fine ... just one of the chaps. But when it comes to relationships ... disaster area really. |
| BARRY | Can't think why. |
| FRAN | Do you know what my worst nightmare would be? Being in a dimly-lit room with a man, with romantic music playing softly in the background. |
| BARRY | I tried that with a girl once. She fell asleep. |
| FRAN | I'd be the opposite. I'd chatter on pointlessly and endlessly until *you* fell asleep. (*Embarrassed.*) Sorry ... when I say *you* ... I'm not suggesting ... |
| BARRY | No, of course not. Wouldn't think of it. Wouldn't work. |
| FRAN | See, there I go. Like a bull in a china shop. It's no wonder I frighten people off! |
| BARRY | No, I mean it wouldn't work because I dropped my iPod in the bath ... no soft music available. |
| FRAN | Just the dim lights then. |
| BARRY | No dimmer switch. I could offer a low energy bulb and a quick strum on a broken banjo though. |
| FRAN | Ah ... sounds more my style. |

BARRY          I could probably run to a take-away curry as
               well ... that's just hypothetical of course ...

FRAN           Yes, of course ... probably never happen.

BARRY          No ... quite.

FRAN           Sounds fun though. And I do like a good
               vindaloo ...

BARRY          Afraid I'm more of a korma man. Still ...
               was thinking of treating myself to a curry
               next weekend actually. I suppose you're
               probably busy.

FRAN           Not really. Are you propositioning me,
               West?

BARRY          I think I must be.

FRAN           Well, you'll certainly be a challenge. Never
               known such a scruffy individual.

               (SIMON *enters from the car park. He is totally*
               *dumbfounded. In shock rather than angry.*)

SIMON          Have you seen my car?

FRAN           'Fraid so.

SIMON          It's supposed to be a five series ... it's
               shorter than a bloomin' one series! I only
               washed it yesterday.

FRAN           Perhaps the water was a bit too hot.

               (BARRY *stifles a guffaw and glances at* FRAN
               *as they share the joke.*)

| | |
|---|---|
| SIMON | (*in his own world*) There's barely ten thousand miles on the clock and it looks like it's been driven by a Frenchman. |
| BARRY | Sorry, Simon. It happened in the accident. |
| SIMON | Accident? Well, it wouldn't surprise me, *Barry*, if you didn't do it on purpose. I mean, you've been off with the wife and drained all the water out of my pond so why stop at that … you might as well go the whole hog and jigger the car as well. Do you know how much that metallic paint finish cost? |
| BARRY | I can explain, Simon. |
| SIMON | Oh yes, you've got some explaining to do alright! I trusted you, Barry … like I trust everybody in this club. And how do you repay that trust … you drive a bloomin' tractor into my car. Is that any way to go on? |
| BARRY | It was only the once. |
| SIMON | And once is enough isn't it. I'll be off the road for weeks. Enough said? Point taken? |
| BARRY | I mean with Laura. |
| SIMON | I've spent hours buffing those alloy wheels and where has it got me. |
| BARRY | Don't you care about Laura? |
| SIMON | (*exploding*) Care? Of course I bloomin' care, man … she's my wife … but I can't worry about *everything* at the same time can I! Have you seen the state of my car? |

(TIFFANY *appears at the doorway to the bar. She sees* SIMON *and looks over at him sadly.*)

TIFFANY      I'm sorry, Simon.

SIMON        And so you jolly well should be. (*With a sudden realisation.*) Who's going to pay for the repairs?

TIFFANY      (*moving to* SIMON, *sympathetic*) No, I mean I'm sorry … really, really sorry. I've just seen Laura, she's on her way.

SIMON        On her way where? (*Turning to* BARRY.) This is all your fault. You've wrecked my car and now you're wrecking my marriage.

TIFFANY      *I* wrecked your car, Simon, but it's not about that. It's about your mother.

SIMON        (*pointing at* BARRY) I suppose he's had *her* as well has he?

TIFFANY      Laura's just had a phone call from the hospital. She was white as a sheet … said it was the worse possible news.

SIMON        What?

TIFFANY      I think you should sit down for a minute.

BARRY        Here, mate.

             (BARRY *stands and takes a chair over to* SIMON. *He puts it down and* SIMON *looks at* BARRY *and the chair warily, as if expecting it to be booby-trapped, before sitting on it.*)

SIMON        (*to* BARRY) Judas.

BARRY               (*sadly*) Yeah.

                    (BARRY *moves back towards* FRAN, *who stands*.)

FRAN                (*to* BARRY) We'll give him a few minutes. I'll buy you that drink. (*To* SIMON.) Sorry, Weaver ... (*Uncertain what to say*.) ... bad luck. (*Looking at* BARRY.) You okay?

BARRY               Fine.

                    (FRAN *hesitantly holds out her hand and* BARRY *takes it, smiling*.)

                    Tell you what, I'll buy *you* a drink.

                    (FRAN *and* BARRY *exit into the bar, hand in hand*. TIFFANY *watches on, open-mouthed*.)

TIFFANY             (*half to herself*) Barry!

SIMON               (*muttering to himself*) I don't believe this ... I just don't believe it. It's a bloomin' conspiracy.

                    (LAURA *appears at the doorway to the bar. She looks dreadful and is obviously coming down from the high of being drunk and starting with the low of a hangover. Throughout the remaining action it is clear that thinking and speaking require painful concentration and effort*.)

LAURA               (*blinking painfully*) God, it's bright out here!

                    (TIFFANY *sees* LAURA *and moves to her*.)

TIFFANY        I sat him down. He's just had a bit of a
               shock ... (*Glancing towards the bar.*) So
               have I actually.

LAURA          Fine.

TIFFANY        I'll just go and keep an eye on Barry.

LAURA          Fine. Absolutely.

               (TIFFANY *exits into the bar.* LAURA *makes
               her way slowly and painfully to one of the
               chairs and sits. During the first part of the
               following conversation,* LAURA *and* SIMON
               *talk to each other, but in a detached way,
               each of them caught up in their personal
               misery.*)

               This wasn't a good idea.

SIMON          I told you not to drink too much but you
               wouldn't listen.

LAURA          Yes, you're always right, darling. All my
               fault as usual. The hospital rang.

SIMON          Yes, I know.

LAURA          Bit out of the blue. Maybe it was inevitable
               but I wasn't really prepared for it.

SIMON          Suppose not. Thing is, it's not fair ... it's
               not fair at all.

LAURA          Life rarely is.

SIMON          I mean, today of all days. And it was all
               going so well. (*Standing and moving to*
               LAURA.) Do you realise it's over twenty

years I've been a member here ... and that's the best score I've ever had.

LAURA          Not that important in the greater scheme of things.

SIMON          Oh, absolutely not ... point taken, Laura ... point absolutely bloomin' well taken. Even so, it would have been nice just for once ... to be up there taking the plaudits. (*Pause.*) It's the first thing I've ever won you know ... in my whole bloomin' life it's the first thing I've won. I could have been up there tonight, giving a speech.

LAURA          So what's stopping you? Virtually every time you open your mouth we get a speech, Simon.

SIMON          What's stopping me? You amaze me sometimes, Laura, you really do. I might have my faults ... small ones ... enough said ... but even I couldn't be so totally crass as to stand up there tonight. She's done it on purpose. Ever since I was a boy she'd find a way to ruin every bit of fun I ever had. I know it's not kind ... not very politically correct ... but I've never liked Mother, Laura ... *loved* but never liked.

LAURA          No point beating yourself up about it.

SIMON          No, I suppose not. (*Pausing sadly and then, with a glimmer of an idea.*) Do you think maybe I *could* get away with it? If I gave her a mention ... turned my speech into a kind of eulogy ... dedicated the victory, etcetera, etcetera. What do you think?

LAURA          Eulogy?

SIMON         We don't have to go off and identify her or
              anything do we?

LAURA         Well I wouldn't have thought so.

SIMON         Do they still stick those labels on peoples
              toes?

LAURA         What on earth are you talking about,
              Simon? She's coming home tomorrow.

SIMON         What? But the girl ... Tiffany ... she said it
              was the worst possible news!

LAURA         So it is ... she's coming home to *us*.

SIMON         Us? Us!

LAURA         They said she can't be left on her own for
              the foreseeable future. I'd have a drink if I
              didn't feel so bloody awful.

SIMON         Us? We'll have to find a Home for her. She's
              not going to be a burden on *you* like that
              ... I won't have it ... I won't. We're a team,
              Laura ... a bloomin' good team, and I won't
              have you put upon.

LAURA         How can we be a team, Simon? We're not
              exactly team players are we? Either of us.

SIMON         Of course we are.

LAURA         But we're never together! You're always
              here and I ... well I won't go into that again
              ... unless you want me to.

SIMON         No, I bloomin' well don't! I don't want to
              labour the point but I think you said quite
              enough earlier on.

LAURA      I didn't mean to but you can be so bloody
           infuriating. Angry?

SIMON      Angry? Of course I'm bloomin' angry! I
           mean, how would you feel if I was ... if I
           was ... carrying on like that?

LAURA      But you wouldn't would you ... not you,
           Simon. It would be bad form wouldn't
           it ... not the done thing ... unacceptable
           behaviour.

SIMON      As it happens there have been occasions
           when the opportunity might have presented
           itself. Young Mrs Elliot took quite a shine
           to me when I gave her some pointers on her
           chip and run technique. I took it no further
           of course ... even though she is one of the
           more shapely members.

LAURA      Really? Well, maybe you should have taken
           advantage of the situation. It might have
           done you some good!

SIMON      And what's that supposed to mean? Just
           because I couldn't ... couldn't give you any
           children ... it doesn't mean I can't ...

LAURA      It's not about that, Simon. It's never been
           about that.

SIMON      No, maybe not ... so you say.

LAURA      Look, none of this was designed to hurt
           you. I just needed something else ...
           something more. It's not as though we've
           exactly been setting the world on fire
           together lately. Can you remember the last
           time we actually went out together?

SIMON        No ... point taken ... message received and
             (*Self-consciously tailing off both his speech
             and his 'mime'.*) ...

LAURA        I'm sorry, Simon. I'm truly sorry.

SIMON        Good ....fine ... apology accepted. Must try
             harder ... (*Only half-joking.*) ... I'll make
             a note. (*Pause.*) But ... I mean, it's not as
             though I didn't know.

LAURA        What? You knew?

SIMON        Not the specifics but I'm not stupid. I know
             things have been ... going on. That you've
             been ... you know.

LAURA        You bastard! You bastard! Why didn't
             you say something? Why didn't you *do*
             something?

SIMON        Didn't seem much point.

LAURA        No point? I can't believe I'm hearing this.
             The whole *point*, Simon, is that I was crying
             out for you to pay me some attention.

SIMON        And what about attention for me, Laura?
             What about me? Ever since we found out
             it was *me* who couldn't have children ....
             it always seemed like ... like I was no use
             to you any more. Couldn't ... fulfil my
             purpose in life.

LAURA        I've never said that. I've never thought
             that! Why didn't you stand up for yourself,
             Simon? If you knew about my affairs why
             not say something?

SIMON            Say something? (*Suddenly blurting out his
                 feelings.*) Alright then ... if you want the
                 truth ... I was frightened ... okay? I was
                 frightened that if I said anything it would
                 force your hand ... make *you* have to make a
                 decision. Is that so bad of me?

LAURA            (*softening*) No, Simon ... no, it isn't.

SIMON            It hasn't been easy, Laura ... knowing. But
                 it was better than the alternative. Don't ask
                 questions, I thought ... give her some space
                 ... don't change the status quo.

LAURA            It's the bloody status quo that's been
                 strangling me!

SIMON            Well ... so now we know. So ... are you
                 leaving me?

LAURA            No, that was never the intention. Are you
                 kicking me out?

SIMON            And all this stuff, with Barry ... and the
                 others.

LAURA            A bit of fun, Simon ... a bit of harmless
                 fun. It never amounted to anything more
                 than that. I do love you, Simon, but you can
                 be a real pain in the arse.

SIMON            Right. Fine. Love you too. Point taken?

LAURA            Is that it?

SIMON            Well it isn't actually, because I can't say
                 that I'm not a bit disappointed, Laura.
                 I mean, Barry of all people! But in the
                 broader context of our team effort I'm
                 prepared to make some allowances for ...

indiscretions … so I won't labour the point.
Now, if you don't mind, we'll defer further
discussion until a later date. This is a big
day for me and I'd like to remain focussed.
Enough said?

LAURA      Point taken. I suppose this isn't the place.
           But if I didn't have this headache I'd come
           over there and give you a good slap.

SIMON      Good. Everything back to normal then.
           (SIMON *moves to* LAURA *and gives her a peck
           on the cheek.*) We *are* a team you know. A
           bloomin' good one.

LAURA      If you say so, darling. We just seem to keep
           dropping the baton.

SIMON      Have you seen what they've done to my car?

LAURA      Tiffany told me. I never did like it anyway
           … bit pretentious.

SIMON      I'm Secretary of a prestigious golf club! I
           can hardly ride around in an old banger.

LAURA      I heard about Nick's bike as well … and the
           bush.

SIMON      Vandalism. (*Sulkily.*) And they're trying to
           diddle me out of nearest the pin.

LAURA      Diddums.

SIMON      Oh, it's alright for you, Laura … you don't
           have to sort it all out.

LAURA      Let's go and get a drink.

| | |
|---|---|
| SIMON | Oh no, I don't think that's wise ... I don't think you're up to it. |
| LAURA | It's alright, I promise I won't shout at the Mayor again. |
| SIMON | He went home in a paddy. |
| LAURA | Good, he looked like an obnoxious little toad. Come on ... hair of the dog. (*Kissing* SIMON.) I meant what I said, Simon. Underneath the huff and the puff you're a good man. I just wish you'd notice *me*. |
| | (LAURA *grabs hold of* SIMON'S *hand and tries to lead him into the bar. He follows her but shakes his hands free.*) |
| SIMON | Not while I'm on official duty ... don't want to set a poor example. |
| | (*As* LAURA *and* SIMON *move towards the bar,* TIFFANY *appears at the doorway dragging* BARRY *out of the bar.*) |
| BARRY | Tiffs, I was just starting to enjoy myself then! |
| TIFFANY | I know ... that's why I dragged you out. (*Noticing* LAURA *and* SIMON *and speaking to them with her 'concerned' expression.*) Alright? It's never as bad as you think ... (*Realizing what she has said.*) ... well, I suppose it is sometimes. |
| LAURA | Everything is fine, Tiffany, thank you. (*Noticing that* BARRY *and* SIMON *are standing stiffly and formally, avoiding eye contact with each other.*) Well aren't you two going to speak? |

SIMON          Why should I?

LAURA          Because I've just told you to.

SIMON          Oh ... right.

BARRY          (*formally*) Simon.

SIMON          (*formally*) Barry.

LAURA          With feeling?

SIMON          (*stiffly*) I don't think that would be
               appropriate under the circumstances.

LAURA          Oh, for goodness sake! (*To* BARRY.) I've
               explained to Simon that we were simply
               having a little harmless fun and he has
               graciously agreed to let bygones be
               bygones.

SIMON          I didn't say that.

LAURA          I know ... you wouldn't have kept it so
               short. Shake hands.

BARRY          (*nodding apologetically and holding out his
               hand*) Sorry, Simon. It wasn't fun really ...

               (LAURA *scowls at him.*)

               ... well, you know what I mean.

               (SIMON *is reluctant to take* BARRY's *hand.*)

LAURA          Simon ... I won't tell you again.

SIMON          (*steeling himself and taking* BARRY's *hand*)
               Apology accepted ... enough said. I would,
               however, like to add ...

| | |
|---|---|
| LAURA | No you wouldn't. |
| | (LAURA *grabs* SIMON'S *hand and drags him in to the bar.*) |
| SIMON | (*as he is dragged away*) Shirt, Barry. |
| TIFFANY | (*to* BARRY) What was all that about? |
| BARRY | (*ruefully, as he tucks his shirt in*) To be honest, Tiffs, I *never* really knew what it was all about. More to the point, what's all *this* about? |
| TIFFANY | What are you doing with Fran, Barry? I can't believe you were doing that in there. |
| BARRY | It was only a kiss. |
| TIFFANY | (*pulling a face*) But that's horrible. I mean I think she's really nice but I don't think you should do that. |
| BARRY | Has Simon recruited you into his morality police? |
| TIFFANY | (*curious*) Wasn't she a bit stubbly? I suppose not, with all the hormone treatment and stuff. |
| | (BARRY *looks at her, totally lost.*) |
| | Surely Nick's told you? |
| BARRY | What? |
| TIFFANY | (*moving closer to him, checking that no one can overhear*) She's a lady-man. |

(BARRY *looks at her as though she is totally mad.*)

(*nodding earnestly*) Honestly. Actually, she's probably three quarters lady because she's had the op and everything, but you want to be careful ... I mean you never know.

BARRY      (*suppressing a laugh*) Do you believe *everything* that Nick tells you?

TIFFANY      No of course not, I know what he's like ... that's why I asked *her* about it.

BARRY      Well, he definitely got you this time.

TIFFANY      I think you're wrong, Barry.

BARRY      But Fran's already shown me the evidence.

TIFFANY      (*wide-eyed*) She hasn't!

BARRY      Wait here a minute. (BARRY *moves to the doorway and calls, beckoning.*) Fran, Nick, have you got a minute? Go and get that photo, Fran.

TIFFANY      Don't, Barry ... I don't want to cause a scene.

BARRY      That's something, coming from someone who's just wiped out half the car park.

(NICK *exits from the bar carrying a drink.*)

NICK      What's all the fuss then?

TIFFANY      Have you been telling me fibs, Nick, because if you have I will *so* be cross.

NICK            What about?

                (FRAN *exits from the bar carrying a framed*
                *photograph. She overhears* TIFFANY'S *next*
                *line.*)

TIFFANY         That Fran's a gentleman.

FRAN            We're all gentlemen, Tiffany, even the girls
                ... officers and gentlemen in the finest
                traditions of the Armed Forces.

BARRY           Show her the photo, Fran.

FRAN            They shouldn't be allowed to put it on
                display like that. It makes me feel ancient.

                (FRAN *holds the framed photo up for*
                TIFFANY *to see it.* TIFFANY *looks at it,*
                *blankly.*)

TIFFANY         What am I looking at?

FRAN            A very old picture of the club's youth
                section. (*Pointing.*) There's Armitage.

TIFFANY         Nick? Look at your little thin arms ...
                it doesn't look like you at all. (*Peering*
                *closely.*) Why's your hair all like that?

NICK            (*embarrassed*) My mother always cut it.

FRAN            And that's me ... with the cup. I beat them
                all that year ... even the chaps.

TIFFANY         You! But you look lovely!

FRAN            (*not sure how to take it*) Thank you.

| | |
|---|---|
| TIFFANY | No, I didn't mean it like that … but you've got a skirt on and everything! |
| NICK | Best looker in the youth section … we all fancied Fran. |
| FRAN | How times have changed eh? |
| BARRY | I wouldn't say that. Pity *I* didn't know you then … I was better looking than Nick. |
| TIFFANY | Nicholas … I am *so* not amused. |
| NICK | (*grinning*) Had you going though didn't I? (*To* FRAN.) She thought you were a feller. |

(FRAN *looks at* TIFFANY *in surprise*.)

| | |
|---|---|
| TIFFANY | I didn't! Honestly … I didn't. |

(LAURA *enters from the bar, followed by* SIMON. *They are both carrying drinks, but* SIMON *is struggling to carry his because he is also frantically trying to jot notes into his notebook*.)

| | |
|---|---|
| LAURA | Come on, Simon, stop dawdling. |
| SIMON | I'm not bloomin' dawdling. I'm trying to write a speech. |
| LAURA | (*impatient*) Here. (LAURA *takes* SIMON's *drink from him and places it on a table*.) There … sit down for goodness sake. |
| SIMON | (*grumbling*) I haven't got long. |

(SIMON *sits and continues scribbling*.)

| | |
|---|---|
| LAURA | (*to the others*) You've created quite a stir. Half the club seem to think you're villains but the rest have you marked down as heroes. |
| SIMON | Yes, but they haven't had their car wrecked. I'm not losing my no-claims. |
| NICK | Neither am I! |
| TIFFANY | You haven't got any, Nick! |
| NICK | That's not the point ... it's the principle. (*Turning on* SIMON.) It wouldn't have happened if you hadn't left the compound unlocked. |
| SIMON | Oh, it's all my fault now is it? |
| BARRY | (*cautiously*) I think technically it might make you partly responsible. |
| SIMON | Don't you start, you ... lothario. |
| LAURA | (*sharply*) Simon, behave yourself. Actually, there's no reason why either of you should be out of pocket. (*To* SIMON.) That's why I brought you out here ... to explain my brilliant plan. |
| SIMON | The last brilliant plan you had was moving house. That cost me a small fortune. |
| LAURA | Don't quibble, Simon. As I understand it there are two areas of contention ... uninsured damage to vehicles and uprooted bush. |
| SIMON | And them diddling me out of nearest the pin. |

LAURA        Let's concentrate on the important issues
             shall we?

             (SIMON *scowls*.)

             Tiffany, did anybody see your little accident
             with the tractor?

TIFFANY      I don't think so ... it was just like ... oops!

LAURA        Problem solved then. It was Simon who was
             driving the tractor.

SIMON        (*standing*) What? I was with you, Laura!

LAURA        You have a dreadful memory, darling. I
             assume that as an officer of the club you
             would be insured to drive it?

SIMON        Yes of course. I have used it on occasions.

LAURA        There you are ... simple. Your car and
             Nick's bike both get fixed.

SIMON        But I couldn't ... I mean that would be
             lying. And people would think that I
             couldn't drive it properly ... oh, no.

LAURA        You could get the little dent in the door
             done as well, where you ran into the
             rockery.

SIMON        No ... absolutely not ... no (*Faltering.*) ... I
             suppose it is a bit unsightly.

TIFFANY      Everybody makes up little extra claims on
             their insurance, Simon.

SIMON        Ah but ... if I was driving, it would make
             me an accessory in the vandalism to the
             bush.

FRAN         But given the split opinion of the members,
             you're damned if you did and damned if
             you didn't, Weaver. You'd have the undying
             gratitude of the lady members.

LAURA        And it would do your image no harm at all.
             God knows it needs a bit of a boost

SIMON        What image?

LAURA        Do you want to be seen as a man of decisive
             action or a petty stickler for the rules?

SIMON        Petty stickler? Oh, no, that's not me at all.
             I've always cut to the core of any situation
             as any of the members will vouch.

FRAN         Absolutely.

BARRY        Very forward thinking.

LAURA        That's settled then.

SIMON        (*wrestling with his conscience*) No ... can't
             do it. As Secretary I must stand for fair play
             and sportsmanship in all matters relating to
             the club. End of the matter I'm afraid.

LAURA        (*sighing and beckoning* SIMON *to her side*) A
             word, darling.

             (SIMON *moves hesitantly to* LAURA'S *side and
             she talks to him quietly.*)

             If we're talking about sportsmanship you
             wouldn't want me to let slip about your

little secret would you ... in the middle of
your speech?

SIMON        What secret?

LAURA        The little draw-string hole you make in the
             pocket of your golfing trousers ... the one
             you use for cheating ... for dropping golf
             balls when you lose them.

SIMON        (*indignant*) I do not ... that's outrageous ...
             that hole's for ... for letting the water drain
             out of my pocket on rainy days.

LAURA        (*shrugging*) Your choice.

             (SIMON *visibly twitches as he wrestles with
             the problem.*)

SIMON        (*reluctantly, turning to the others*) After a
             short period of recuperation, the haze of
             amnesia that afflicted me after the impact
             of the collision is now clearing. It seems
             to me that I was in fact the driver of the
             tractor.

BARRY        Very unfortunate, the way your foot slipped
             off the brake like that.

NICK         Hardly your fault ... could happen to
             anyone.

SIMON        Of course, I was merely assisting you in
             taking urgent action after you spotted
             the critically dangerous condition of the
             bush. It could have toppled at any moment
             causing a threat to life and limb.

LAURA        And you win nearest the pin, Barry. An
             apology from me. Is that fair?

| | |
|---|---|
| BARRY | (*smiling*) Absolutely. |
| SIMON | Oh no, hang on, Laura ... there are limits. |
| LAURA | (*smiling sweetly at* SIMON) Remember your balls, Simon. |
| SIMON | (*gritting his teeth and turning back to the others*) Congratulations, Barry. Well done. Good shot. |
| BARRY | (*beaming happily*) Have I won something nice? |
| NICK | New driver, so I'll accept it back as a replacement for the one you broke. You could pay me the hundred quid instead of course. |
| FRAN | (*to* BARRY) Don't you dare give him a penny, West ... he's a rogue ... always has been. |
| BARRY | Aren't you going to call me Barry now? |
| FRAN | Absolutely not. Doesn't suit. Come on, West ... we should be getting changed for dinner. |
| | (FRAN *and* BARRY *exit into the bar.*) |
| LAURA | Speech all ready, darling? |
| SIMON | (*looking at his notebook*) Think so. |
| NICK | It's not going to be a long one is it, Simon ... we want to enjoy ourselves. |
| SIMON | Oh, just a few well chosen observations ... as you know I'm a man of few words, Nicholas. Short ... succinct ... I'll not labour the point ... enough said? But I |

wouldn't mind just running a little passage past you all ... delicate part ... just want to make sure I hit the mark ...

(SIMON *flicks through a couple of pages in his notebook to find the correct place.*)

TIFFANY        (*to* NICK) Can't you stop him, Nick ... he *so* does my head in.

SIMON          Ah, here we are ... (*Reading, adopting a grave stance and tone. As he reads,* LAURA *rolls her eyes in disbelief.*) 'Ladies and Gentlemen, few of you will be aware of the grave personal tragedy which haunted me as I fought for this trophy. But indeed, a giant sword of Damocles has been hovering over me throughout the day. With your forbearance, therefore, I would like to humbly dedicate this victory to my dear, much loved mother, who, even as I speak, lies critically ill in hospital ...

(FRAN *appears at the door to the bar.*)

FRAN           I think a few more may be joining her, Weaver. We'll have to cancel the dinner I'm afraid.

SIMON          What? But we can't! It's the biggest day of my golfing life.

FRAN           Dropping like flies ... huge queue for the loos. Looks like food poisoning.

(*They all slowly turn to look at* TIFFANY.)

TIFFANY        (*smiling weakly*) Oops!

(*The lights fade.*)

## FURNITURE AND PROPERTY LIST

### ACT 1 SCENE 1

| | |
|---|---|
| Set | Two patio tables, four patio chairs, golf balls on putting green. |
| Personal | Putter, handkerchief (Barry)<br>Notebook and pencil, mobile phone (Simon)<br>Motorcycle helmet, motorcycle gloves (Nick) |
| Offstage | Box of putting green flags (Simon)<br><br>Folded table, closed cardboard box, cardboard box with collapsible bottom containing bags of 'squashy sausages' etc. (Tiffany) |

### ACT 1 SCENE 2

| | |
|---|---|
| Strike | Putter, folded table, motorcycle helmet, motorcycle gloves. |
| Set | Re-position one table and new unfolded table covered by tablecloth on putting green. Tables on putting green to be loaded with a camping stove with kettle and frying pan containing half cooked sausages, putting green flag, bread rolls, sandwiches, pies, cucumber, tea bags, coffee jar, orange squash, plastic beakers and plates, napkins, sauce sachets and various card board boxes. Tiffany's shoes under the table. |
| Personal | Hand written note (Tiffany)<br>Score card and pencil (Nick)<br>Score card and pencil (Fran)<br>Score card and pencil (Barry)<br>Notebook and pencil, keys (Simon)<br>Handbag (Laura) |
| Offstage | Spade, glass of gin and tonic (Simon)<br>Chocolate bar (Tiffany) |

## ACT 2 SCENE 1

Set | Re-position one patio table on which are placed empty bottle of wine, glass of wine, magazine and two empty gin glasses. On other patio table place used plates, napkins and beakers. Rearrange 'debris' on folding table. Reposition three chairs.

Personal | Cucumber slices over eyes (Tiffany)
Sun glasses (Laura)
Notebook and pencil, mobile phone (Simon)

Offstage | Large gin and tonic (Laura)

## ACT 2 SCENE 2

Strike | Everything except two patio tables and four patio chairs.

Set | Re-position tables and chairs. Pint glass containing a small quantity of beer on one of the tables.

Personal | Safety helmet and gloves (Fran)
Nike golf ball (Barry)
Handbag containing packet of tablets (Tiffany)
Notebook and pencil (Simon)

Offstage | Framed photograph (Fran)
Gin and tonic (Laura)
Glass of beer (Simon)

## LIGHTING PLOT

Bright sunshine throughout.

## EFFECTS PLOT

| Cue 1 | Page 1  | *Harley Davidson* |
|-------|---------|-------------------|
| Cue 2 | Page 18 | *Mobile phone ring* |
| Cue 3 | Page 34 | *Golf ball being hit* |
| Cue 4 | Page 36 | *Golf ball being hit, followed by shout of "fore left" followed by sound of breaking glass* |
| Cue 5 | Page 37 | *Golf ball being hit, followed by shout of "fore right"* |

# Par for the Course - Set - Proscenium Stage

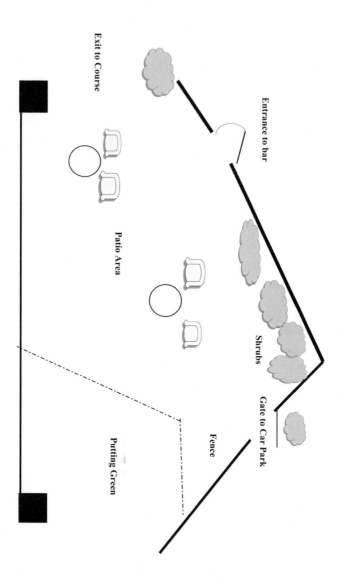

Exit to Course

Entrance to bar

Patio Area

Shrubs

Gate to Car Park

Fence

Putting Green